ONCE AGAIN

The Witches' Almanac

SPRING 1998 — SPRING 1999

For the first time combining the mysterious wiccan and arcane
secrets of an old England witch with one from New England

Prepared and edited by
ELIZABETH PEPPER and JOHN WILCOCK

CONTAINING pictorial and explicit delineations of the magical phases of
the Moon together with full and complete information about astrological
portents of the year to come and various aspects of occult knowledge
enabling all who read to improve their lives in the old manner.

The Witches' Almanac, Ltd.

Publishers   Newport

Address all inquiries and information to
THE WITCHES' ALMANAC, LTD.
P.O. Box 4067
Middletown, Rhode Island 02842

ISBN: 0-88496-426-4

First Printing January 1998

Printed in the United States of America

Preface

An old riddle asks, "Which is greater—the oak tree or the dandelion?" The answer: "Whichever one fulfills its potential." Some say self-fulfillment is an inferior motive, and to devote your life to some higher cause is the more worthy endeavor. Yet if you deny a mysterious spirit dwelling within you, you serve no one and are actually cheating yourself.

There's a spark of creative energy in every one of us. You can accept it, ignore it, or fan it into a flame. The choice is yours. The expression of your sacred gift is completely unique. If you should fail to develop it, become discouraged, or bend to the judgement of others, it will never exist. Society's winds are strong and many a candle gutters out before it can become a sure and steady flame. Cherish your light. Determine to protect and maintain its glow from all the remote and impersonal forces that may threaten to extinguish it.

Witchcraft relies on nature to guide and comfort the spirit. Observe the world around you. Take time to enjoy the beauty of dawn and twilight, the silent procession of clouds and stars crossing the sky. There's peace and delight to be found in their constancy amidst change. Imagination is quickened by the colors, rhythm, and harmony concealed within the ever-shifting patterns. You are part of nature. It is part of you.

HOLIDAYS

Spring 1998 to Spring 1999

March 20	Vernal Equinox
April 1	All Fools' Day
April 30	Beltane Eve
May 1	Roodmas
May 8	White Lotus Day
May 9, 11, 13	Lemuria
May 29	Oak Apple Day
June 5	Night of the Watchers
June 20	Midsummer Night
June 21	Summer Solstice
June 24	St. John's Day
July 31	Lughnassad Eve
August 1	Lammas
August 13	Diana's Day
August 29	Day of Thoth
September 22	Autumnal Equinox
October 31	Samhain Eve
November 1	Hallowmas
November 16	Hecate Night
December 17	Saturnalia
December 21	Winter Solstice
January 9	Feast of Janus
February 1	Oimelc Eve
February 2	Candlemas
March 1	Matronalia

CONTENTS

ELIZABETH PEPPER & JOHN WILCOCK
Executive Editors

KERRY CUDMORE
Managing Editor

JEAN MARIE WALSH
Associate Editor

Astrologer	Dikki-Jo Mullen
Climatologist	Tom C. Lang
Contributing Editor	Barbara Stacy
Production	Bendigo Associates
Sales	Ellen Murphy

Lines from *L'Allegro*

And ever, against eating cares,
Lap me in soft Lydian airs,
Married to immortal verse,
Such as the meeting soul may pierce
In notes with many a winding bout
Of linkéd sweetness long drawn out,
With wanton heed and giddy cunning,
The melting voice through mazes running,
Untwisting all the chains that tie
The hidden soul of harmony.

— JOHN MILTON
1608-1674

The Celestial Sphere   Erhard Schon, 1515

The Earth was the center of the universe according to Claudius Ptolemy of
Alexandria, who wrote the first astrological textbook in 150 A.D.

MOON GARDENING

BY PHASE

Sow, transplant, bud and graft   *Plow, cultivate, weed and reap*

NEW	First Quarter	FULL	Last Quarter	NEW
Plant above-ground crops with outside seeds, flowering annuals.	Plant above-ground crops with inside seeds.		Plant root crops, bulbs, biennials, perennials.	Do not plant.

BY PLACE IN THE ZODIAC

Fruitful Signs

Cancer - Most favorable planting time for all leafy crops bearing fruit above ground. Prune to encourage growth in Cancer.

Scorpio - Second only to Cancer, a Scorpion Moon promises good germination and swift growth. In Scorpio, prune for bud development.

Pisces - Planting in the last of the Watery Triad is especially effective for root growth.

Taurus - The best time to plant root crops is when the Moon is in the sign of the Bull.

Capricorn - The Earthy Goat Moon promotes the growth of rhizomes, bulbs, roots, tubers and stalks. Prune now to strengthen branches.

Libra - Airy Libra may be the least beneficial of the Fruitful Signs, but is excellent for planting flowers and vines.

Barren Signs

Leo - Foremost of the Barren Signs, the Lion Moon is the best time to effectively destroy weeds and pests. Cultivate and till the soil.

Gemini - Harvest in the Airy Twins; gather herbs and roots. Reap when the Moon is in a sign of Air or Fire to assure best storage.

Virgo - Plow, cultivate, and control weeds and pests when the moon is in Virgo.

Sagittarius - Plow and cultivate the soil or harvest under the Archer Moon. Prune now to discourage growth.

Aquarius - This dry sign of Air is perfect for ground cultivation, reaping crops, gathering roots and herbs. It is a good time to destroy weeds and pests.

Aries - Cultivate, weed, and prune to lessen growth. Gather herbs and roots for storage.

Consult our Moon Calendar pages for phase and place in the zodiac circle. The Moon remains in a sign for about two-and-a-half days. Match your gardening activity to the day that follows the Moon's entry into that zodiac sign.

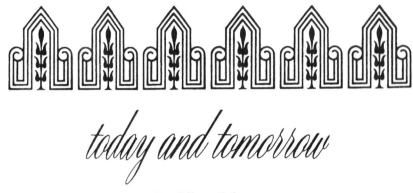

today and tomorrow

By Oliver Johnson

DENTAL DONATIONS: The Tooth Fairy has been getting more generous lately, leaving an average payment of $1.75 under pillows compared with $1 earlier in the decade—an increase roughly equivalent to the rate of inflation. These figures come from a recent national poll conducted by St. Louis dentist William Hartel, who reveals that the rate appears to be pretty constant for both rich and poor families. "A child who loses a tooth has to come to an understanding of what's going on, both practically in terms of chewing and in (losing)…part of the body," explains psychologist Michael Schwartzman. He adds, "The Tooth Fairy is a warm, giving maternal figure who helps children accept and feel

good about what happened." The custom has endured, suggests Rosemary Wells—a self-titled Tooth Fairy Consultant—because it helps both parent and child through a stressful situation. Wells, a former English professor, operates the Tooth Fairy Museum out of her Deerfield, Illinois home, which displays 500 items of memorabilia, including buttons, glass figurines, and baseball cards. "Any item that is important to a child can be left by the Tooth Fairy," Wells explains.

ARMORED MAIDEN: A lightweight suit of armor made of 15th-century metal and believed to have been worn by Joan of Arc has been discovered by a Parisian art dealer who found it perfectly fit his teenage daughter. It bears battle scars corresponding to the wounds known to have been suffered by the diminutive Maid of Orleans, who was burned at the stake in 1431 at the age of eighteen. Whether or not there was any truth in the accusations of witchcraft leveled against her is still being debated. But the Lorraine area from which she came had long been

steeped in mysticism, and Joan's life came to be identified with the "marvellous maid" that Merlin (according to historian Geoffrey of Monmouth) predicted would appear in this region. After hearing mysterious voices that commanded her to save France, Joan became a protégée of Charles II, who instructed his armorer to construct a suit of armor to "exactly fit her body." The suit discovered recently has a ribbed breastplate which corresponds to one worn by Joan in a medieval portrait.

PRISON PAGANS: Acceding to pressure from a body known as the "Pagan Federation," Britain's Home Office has accepted paganism as a genuine faith and added it to the list of religions that prisoners can practice in jail. In addition to the solstices and equinoxes, pagans observe Oimelc (Candlemas), Beltane (May Day), Lammas, the first harvest and Samhain, better known as Halloween. Author Philip Heselton, a conservation officer with Hull City Council, has been making 90-minute "chaplain-style" visits with prisoners who worship such old Celtic deities as Ceridwen, the goddess of inspiration, whom Heselton suggests can offer hope for the future to those inside. "I believe our way of going about things is the natural, straightforward approach to our relationship with the earth," he declares.

ORGANIZING ENERGY: The practice of *feng shui* (from the Chinese symbols for "wind" and "water") has been getting increasing attention lately, partly because an influx of Asian immigrants have brought with them the ancient belief that energy should have its appropriate setting. Practitioners believe that people are affected by their relationship to their surroundings and that one's health, prosperity, and luck are determined by living in harmony with the unseen energy called *chi*. The rhythms of the earth are similar to those of the human body, suggests anthropologist Gary Seaman, and for centuries the Chinese have seen both *feng shui* and acupuncture develop side by side—both, according to Seaman, being a form of medicine. The Dallas Morning News reports that Asian banks

Chinese character for *Chi*

have spent millions to assure that their buildings have proper *feng shui*. Every *feng shui* master has stories of people whose lives changed dramatically after they rearranged their homes.

LIBRARY BROUHAHA: Lectures on tarot reading, numerology, and dream analysis would seem to be pretty innocuous, but just the announcement that they were to be held in the local library got the Christian folk of a New Hampshire town up in arms. The Rev. Andrew Gosnell, minister of a Congregational church in Seabrook (population 7,000), alerted his flock who threatened to picket if the lectures were held. Some complained that lectures on the occult simply don't belong in the library, but a counter-petition signed by 250 residents agreed with Teresa Amato. She declared, "The library is the place for controversy. Democracy depends on it and on the free flow of information, not denying people the right to make their own choices." Although the library board bowed to pressure and decided to cancel the lectures, there was an unexpected twist to events. An astrologer in a nearby town publicized the controversy on the Internet and suggested that sympathizers send works on the occult for the library's shelves. Librarian Elizabeth Heath reports, "The response has been overwhelming."

BELTANE BONFIRE: More than 15,000 pagan followers are expected to climb Edinburgh's Calton Hill in Scotland to celebrate the May Eve holiday. The annual festival celebrates its 10th anniversary this year after its revival by a collective known as "the White Warrior Women." As ritual bodyguards to the new May Queen, they lead the celebrants in what has become a major fixture in Edinburgh's cultural calendar. Although the key elements in the revived ceremony are still the symbolic death and rebirth of the Green Man, the kindling of a giant bonfire and the triple clockwise circling of the fire, other elements have

gradually been added over the years. Now the procession incorporates Japanese-style banners and kites, squads of drummers, African totems, and large-scale puppetry. "The energy of Beltane today comes basically from the people who get involved and what they bring to it," explains one of the regular participants.

BIRDS BEWARE: Nobody knows when or where scarecrows were invented, but they have entered the folklore and farming practices of many countries, writes Jenny McClean in The London Times. They were first documented by a writer in the 16th century and were mentioned by both Edmund Spenser in *The Faerie Queene* and by Shakespeare, who called the scarecrows "Jack-a-lents." They have taken many different forms, from the simple plastic bag flapping on a stick to an elaborate motorized robot with flashing eyes and a revolving head installed by a mechanically minded Essex farmer. Gnomes, witches, and clowns have been big favorites over the years, but today's scarecrows— like almost everything else—have finally entered the realm of show business. In Wimborne, Dorset, artist Joyce Warren has created lookalikes in the form of Charlie Chaplin, Ringo Starr,

David Hockney, and Queen Elizabeth. Mrs. Warren works to order, and some of her commissions come from as far away as Japan. "You could say I'm really hung up on scarecrows," she explains. "They are a great tradition, a living thing; the straw just seems to come alive when you start working on one."

BLESS THE BEASTS: Beauty is in the eye of the beholder, but unfortunately the finer points of some creatures aren't appreciated as much as they should be. Some species of snakes and toads were almost on the verge of extinction in recent years until the growing conservation movement started to change public perceptions. The foul appearance of the natterjack toad, for example, caused the mistaken belief that it caused warts and was an instrument of witchcraft. "I don't think they are ugly," says Tony Gent, an official of the ecological group English Nature. "It depends on your perception of life. If you are a toad, you'll think they are very attractive."

A P O L L O

Of Apollo we sing, the Brilliant One, god of sunlight, god of music.

And more glittering powers, as complex and multiple as any deity commanded on Mt. Olympus. He was the god of poetry and dance, painting and sculpture, science and philosophy, the protector of cities and colonies, herds and flocks. The god of youth, Apollo was depicted with golden curls and ravishing androgynous beauty, usually with a lyre and often with arrows as patron of hunters.

And perhaps most important, the god of prophecy. His most celebrated shrine, one of the mightiest Greek sanctuaries, was at Delphi, sited in a deep cavern from which "emanated prophetic vapors," according to one source.

Accounts of the sanctuary echo down the ages, notable in both myth and history. The most bizarre myth—that the center of the cave was the *axis mundi*, the center of the world. At this site rested a large circular netlike relic, the "naval stone" or *omphalos*, flanked by two golden eagles. The birds alluded to the belief that Zeus had marked the midpoint by releasing the eagles from opposite ends of the earth and signifying where beak met beak.

The relic was guarded by Pytho, a monstrous serpent terrorizing the countryside. Apollo slew Pytho—a Greek version of the universal hero/dragon myth—and purified himself from the kill by nine years of exile. Upon his return, Apollo established the site as his own sanctuary and installed a prophetic high priestess, the ambiguous Delphic oracle.

That's one story. Another claims that Apollo took over the Delphic cult and its priestesses, the Sybils, from his grandmother Phoebe, the Shining One, third in succession of the female deities to have oracles at the cavern. Feminists focus on this version, according as it does with the historical argument that a patriarchal culture engulfed an earlier goddess-centered religion, now lost.

The Delphic high-priestess, known as the Pythia, sat on a tall three-legged stool at the cavern's entrance and answered visitors' questions. Predictions flew from her mouth in a frenzy of ravings the Greeks believed were divinely inspired prophesies, although often not readily understood. The location was further memorialized by the Pythiads in Apollo's honor, great athletic games held every four years and rivaled only by the nine-year cycle of Olympics.

Such a magnificent god implies magnificent lineage, and indeed he had. Mighty Zeus himself was Apollo's father, his mother the Titaness Leto. He was born on the island of Delos, twin to the revered Artemis, goddess of the hunt and as associated with the Moon as Apollo was with the Sun. High magic attended at their very birth, for moments after Artemis emerged from the womb she helped her mother give birth to Apollo. The twins remained close companions, often hunting together with their enchanted golden bows and attended by nymphs required to be virgins.

Apollo's lyre was also golden, and from its strings emerged ravishing harmonies. On occasion his musicianship was challenged, and he exacted horrendous penalties for such hubris. When the satyr Marsyas dared to suggest a musical contest, flute against lyre, Apollo handily won—and flayed Marsyas alive for his presumption. The god also engaged in a similar contest with Pan, pipes against lute, and again Apollo won. King Midas, who witnessed the event, dissented and declared that Pan's rustic airs were more lovely. Apollo, appalled by such de-

13

praved taste, caused Midas to grow asses' ears.

The god had many loves, both male and female, but despite his radiance all affairs of the heart seemed to range from luckless to disastrous. Daphne was his first love, evoked by the malice of Cupid. When Apollo saw the son of Venus playing with arrows, he rebuked the child for playing with warlike weapons. Cupid responded by drawing from his quiver two arrows, a gold one to excite love, a lead one to repel it. With the gold arrow he shot Apollo through the heart; with the other, he shot the nymph Daphne.

Apollo pleaded for her love, but she took flight—and even as she fled, she charmed him. "The wind blew her garments, and her unbound hair streamed loose behind her," the mythologist Bullfinch assures us. "So flew the god and the virgin, he on the wings of love, and she on those of fear." In a panic, Daphne called upon her father, a river god, to save her. "Scarcely had she spoken when a stiffness seized all her limbs; her bosom began to be en-

closed in a tender bark; her hair became leaves; her arms became branches; her foot stuck fast in the ground, as a root; her face became a tree-top." The nymph had been changed into a laurel tree, and Apollo, amazed, kissed the bark tenderly. He declared that forever the laurel would be sacred, honored as his crown and as a wreath for heroes. The story inspired a festival, the Daphnephoria or "bringing the laurel," featuring sprigs of the tree in initiation rites for young men "dressed as Apollo"—that is, nude.

As for male lovers, Apollo was most passionate about Hyacinthus. The two were inseparable, and for the beautiful youth Apollo neglected his arrows and his lyre. One day they played quoits, and Apollo heaved the discus high and far. Hyacinthus, excited with the sport, ran forward to seize it, eager to make his own throw. The discus struck him on the forehead and he fell. Apollo struggled to staunch the flow of blood, but the wounded youth's life flickered away, even beyond the skill of the god of healing. Apollo was devastated and swore that Hyacinthus would remain alive in story and song. "My lyre shall celebrate thee, my song shall tell thy fate, and thou shalt become a flower." When Apollo spoke, the blood on the ground beneath the youth's head ceased to be blood, but flowers that return every spring to remind us of Apollo's beloved.

The cult of Apollo at Delphi had an amazingly long run. Historians believe that it was established by the 8th century B.C., but may have been much older. Prophesies flowed from the site until 394 A.D., when the Roman Christian emperor Theodosius the Great shut it down.

Today an ancient replica of the original improbable naval stone rests in a museum at Delphi, a wrinkled reminder of over a thousand years of Apollonian sacrament and eerie glory.

—BARBARA STACY

At Delphi in 1893, French archaeologists unearthed two large marble tablets. A hymn to Apollo, composed in 278 B.C., was engraved on them:

I will sing in praise of thee,
*   glorious son of Zeus!*
Who dwellest on the snowy peak of the hill,
*   where in sacred oracles to mortal men*
Thou dost proclaim tidings prophetic,
*   from the divine tripodic seat.*
Thou hast driven forth from his place
*   the dragon who watched over the shrine,*
And, with thy darts, hast forced him to hide
*   far in the dark underwood.*

Muses come from deeply wooded Helicon,
Beautiful fair-armed daughters of the
*   loud-singing god, dwelling there;*
Praising their noble kinsman, even Phoebus,
*   with golden hair,*
To the lyre they sing their songs.
He hovers o'er the twin-headed peak of
*   Parnasse, and he haunts the rocky places,*
Round about famous Delphi and Castalia's
*   plentiful springs, full of waters deep and clear,*
And presides o'er Delphi with its oracle
*   true in prophecy.*

Illustrations are from *Quaint Cuts in the Chapbook Style* by Joseph Crawhall, published by Dover Publications, Inc., 31 East 2nd St., Mineola, N.Y. 11501

𝔒𝔩𝔡𝔢 𝔈𝔫𝔤𝔩𝔦𝔰𝔥 ℭ𝔥𝔞𝔭𝔟𝔬𝔬𝔨𝔰

For at least a hundred years after Johannes Gutenberg introduced movable type to Europe, books remained—as they had been in the days of medieval manuscripts—a luxury available only to the rich. By the 16th century advances in printing had increased the number of people who could read and write, and there arose a natural market for cheap mass-market literature. It was at this time that the chapbook appeared.

Chapbooks were usually printed on one sheet which when folded would provide a booklet of 8 to 24 pages, depending on the size of the sheet. It was often sold as a flat page, requiring the purchaser to fold, cut, and pin the pages together. The finished booklet, about 6" x 4", was illustrated with crude but lively woodcuts, which were used over and over again and didn't necessarily relate to the subject at hand. Usually chapbooks were undated so they could be sold for years, and they rarely bore an author's name. Much of this early publishing was devoted to the garish reporting of such matters as highway robberies, murders, pirates, blackmail, trials, and cattle stealing; themes such as fortunetelling, dream interpretation, and witchcraft became quite popular as well.

By the late 17th century, chapbooks had become the principal reading matter of the poor. They were usually sold for a penny by traveling peddlers—chapmen—whose stock-in-trade included pins, needles, thimbles, combs, medicines, and all the little items out of reach of the rural poor in the days when the only shops to be found were in towns. The origin of the

word *chapman* is doubtful, but probably derived from the Old English *ceap* meaning "trade."

The early chapman, a long pack suspended from his neck containing his wares, was a hawker often regarded with suspicion. He was chased by the dogs and slept with the pigs or in the barn, but his presence was usually welcome not only for his goods but as a provider of gossip and news of other communities.

Fortunetelling chapbooks carried recipes of love powders to add to the drinks of potential suitors. Mother Bunch's *Golden Fortune Teller* explained the art of divination by tea leaves and coffee grounds; Partridge and Flamstead's *New and Well Experienced Fortune Book* explained the significance of moles, the interpretation of dreams, and fortunetelling by cards.

Mother Shipton, reputedly the daughter of a necromancer who lived in a cave at Knaresborough in Yorkshire, was the subject of innumerable pamphlets which printed her prophecies; the most famous of which predicted the Great Fire of London in 1666. Supposedly she many times recovered property stolen from her neighbors by naming the thieves. Her tombstone reads:

Here lies she who seldom ly'd
Whose skill so often has been try'd:
Her prophecies shall still survive,
And ever keep her name alive.

Another soothsayer was Sir Thomas Learmant of Fyfe, who became known as "Thomas the Rhymer" be-

cause of the way he phrased his predictions. In addition to forecasting storms, Thomas often devoted himself ambiguously to political matters. "The pride of Spain, and the deceitful conduct of the French, as also concerning the Dutch, is all foretold…" he wrote on one occasion.

In 1543 the religionists, alarmed at some of the messages being conveyed, managed to get a proclamation

issued against "foolish books, ballads, rhymes, and other lewd treatises in the English tonge."

Familiar characters such as Robin Hood, Baron Munchausen, Aladdin, Cinderella, Little Red Riding Hood, King Arthur, and Dick Whittington all made regular appearances in chapbooks, and humor was rife with such titles as the 1786 *The Frisky Jester: or, a feast of laughter for the comical fellows; being such a collection of wit and humor as far exceed anything of the kind hitherto published, consisting of humorous jests, smart repartees, pleasant stories, funny jokes, comical adventures and entertaining humbugs.*

In time, chapbooks began to offer their readers a bit of social guidance, frequently advising on written communications. *The Fashionable Letter Writer* sets forth the type of correspondence that should take place between a gentleman and a widow, a daughter and her mother, or a tenant and his landlord. In the 17th century "valentine writers" made their appearances

with books of amorous messages to send to loved ones. One group, called "Quizzical Valentine Writers," even produced satirical or humorous verses suitable for sending to policemen, drunkards, and cuckolds.

Germany, France, the Netherlands, Spain, and China all had their chapbooks. And, as in Europe, the early peddlers in America eventually supplemented their wares with broadsides from colonial printers. Many of the peddlers came from Connecticut and sold thousands of copies of *The New England Primer*, although after 1750 such religious tracts were diluted with chapbooks about scores of other subjects, many of which initially were imported from England. The various tract societies, some of which employed their own agents to travel the country, offered all kinds of religious works.

Parson Weems, a Maryland clergyman best known for his invention of the George Washington cherry tree tale, extensively covered the area between New York and Georgia until his death in 1825 selling bibles, hymn books, and moral tracts written by himself. Due to the prevalence of local newspapers and the various tract societies, chapbooks never achieved the widespread popularity in America that they enjoyed in Britain.

Today, it's difficult to imagine a time when the appearance of the chapman across the fields would be met with such anticipation. But in his day, he and his chapbooks provided a welcome source of news and entertainment, along with something more important—contact and a sense of community with the otherwise unreachable outside world.

The lantern is like the body which encompasses
the soul; the soul within is the light and the part of
it that comprehends and thinks should be ever
open and clear-sighted, and should never be closed
nor remain unseen.

— PLUTARCH
A.D. 46-120

The MOON *Calendar*

is divided into zodiac signs rather than the more familiar Gregorian calendar.

1998

1999

Bear in mind that new projects should be initiated when the Moon is waxing (from dark to full); when the Moon is on the wane (from full to dark), it is a time for storing energy and the wise person waits.

Please note that Moons are listed by day of entry into each sign. Quarters are marked, but as rising and setting times vary from one region to another, it is advisable to check your local newspaper, library or planetarium.

The Moon's Place is computed for Eastern Standard Time.

The Wind   Philip Hagreen, 1921

WIND SONG

Wind and witchcraft are akin. Witch lore records the tale of a medieval Finnish witch who sold wind to becalmed sailors bound up in three knots of rope. The first knot unloosed a gentle breeze; the second brought forth a gale; the third, a tempest. Estonian witches were said to thrust a knife into a block of wood from the direction they wished a wind to blow.

In Scotland the witch, with proper ceremony, could raise the wind by dipping a rag in a fast-moving brook and then beating it three times on a square stone while chanting:

Upon this stone I knock a rag
To raise the wind in the Lady's name,
It shall not lie or cease or die
Until I please again.

English witches could whistle up the wind. In the first light of dawn, facing the point of the compass from which they wished the wind to come, they would summon it with three long, clear whistles blown between the first and fourth fingers of the right hand.

There's a magic moment when witches first realize—know beyond a shadow of a doubt—that they belong to the Craft. Many say their calling came as a voice in the wind.

Among Aradia's gifts of power to the witch, as recounted in Charles G. Leland's translation of the *Vangelo della-Streghe,* or Gospel of the Witches, is the ability to understand the voice of the wind. The symbolic meaning is clear. The motion of human affairs—thoughts, opinions, values—are like the winds: they rise, shift, fall, back and veer; they prevail for a while, freshen into gales only to die again. Change alone endures, and change is the essence of witchcraft.

Casting a spell or making a wish initiates change. When ritual is matched to nature in the form of the winds, the chances of success are markedly increased. There's a wind for every purpose under the sun.

The EAST WIND belongs to new ventures and blesses ambition with energy. Call upon it for courage, patience, and clarity.

The SOUTH WIND favors love, imagination, and fulfillment. Use it in love enchantments and to achieve harmony in close relationships.

The WEST WIND erases doubt, guilt, fear, envy, and hate. It will renew confidence and restore hope.

The NORTH WIND brings with it wisdom. It transcends the other winds as a source of spiritual strength. It protects and increases intuition and divinatory power.

aries | **March 21- April 20**

Mars | *Cardinal Sign of Fire*

s	m	т	w	т	ʄ	s
					1998 Vernal Equinox	Mar. **21** Capricorn
22 *Choose solitude*	**23** Aquarius	**24** *Harry Houdini born, 1874*	**25** Pisces	**26** *Reveal nothing*	**27** Aries	**28** WAXING *Play, laugh, frolic*
29 *Believe in yourself* Taurus	**30**	**31** *Whistle up the wind* Gemini	Apr. **1** All Fool's Day	**2** *Keep moving on* Cancer	**3**	**4** *Trust your intuition*
5 *Set clocks ahead one hour* Leo	**6**	**7** *Maintain pace* Virgo	**8**	**9** *Accept the challenge* Libra	**10** *Make the most of today*	**11** seed moon
12 WANING Scorpio	**13**	**14** *Loretta Lynn born, 1935* Sagittarius	**15**	**16**	**17** *Time is the healer* Capricorn	**18** *Shift your pattern*
19	**20** *The wind is green* Aquarius					

Ancient Italian tomb drawing found at the necropolis in Vulci.

ROMAN HOLIDAYS
Lemuria

The ancients supposed that the souls after death wandered all over the world, and disturbed the peace of its inhabitants. The good spirits were called *Lares familiares*, and the evil ones were known by the name *Larvae*, or *Lemures*. They terrified the good, and continually haunted the wicked and impious; and the Romans celebrated festivals in their honor called *Lemuria* in the month of May. They were first instituted by Romulus to appease the ghost of his brother Remus, from whom they were called *Remuria*, and by corruption, *Lemuria*. These solemnities continued three nights, during which the temples of the gods were shut and marriages prohibited. It was usual for the people to throw black beans on the graves of the deceased, or to burn them, as the smell was supposed to be insupportable to them. They also muttered magical words, and, by beating kettles and drums, they believed that the ghosts would depart and no longer come to terrify their relations upon earth.

A Classical Dictionary
J. Lempriere, 1911

taurus April 21- May 21

Venus   *Fixed Sign of Earth*

s	m	т	w	т	f	s
		Apr. 21 *Ask no questions*	22 *Allow for error* Pisces	23	24 *Check the compass* Aries	25 *Keep your word*
26 ⬤ Taurus	27 WAXING	28 *Test your courage* Gemini	29	30 Eve of Beltane Cancer	May 1 ROODMAS	2 *An old fox smiles* Leo
3 ◑	4 *The caravan moves on* Virgo	5	6 *Orson Welles born, 1915*	7 *Make a clean break* Libra	8 White Lotus Day	9 Lemuria Scorpio
10 *Identify hostile spirit*	11 (hare moon)	12 WANING Sagittarius	13 *Fear kills love*	14 Capricorn	15 *Observe clouds*	16 *Fate can be unkind*
17 *Maureen O'Sullivan born, 1911* Aquarius	18	19 ◑ Pisces	20 *Beware of the backlash*	21 *Hold your tongue* Aries		

25

MIDSUMMER NIGHT LOVE FEAST

Preparing food to share with someone you love is a source of pure delight. Let this magical evening be the occasion of a love feast to honor that most noble emotion.

Curried Chicken Salad

1 chicken breast, halved
1/2 cup green and red grapes
1 tsp. curry powder
1/4 cup mayonnaise
1/2 cup canned mandarin oranges

Place chicken in boiling spring water, lower heat and simmer for about 20 minutes, or until cooked through. Drain, cool and cut into bite-sized chunks. Cut grapes in half and mix curry powder into mayonnaise. Combine chicken and mayonnaise, add grapes, reserving a few for garnish, and mix thoroughly. Gently fold in mandarin orange slices, saving a few for decoration. Chill.

Serve on romaine lettuce. Garnish with an even number of grapes and orange slices. A loaf of crusty bread, sliced at table, accompanies the dish.

Asparagus Tips and Grapefruit

1 lb. asparagus
1 large grapefruit, pink or white
1/4 cup balsamic vinegar
1 tsp. extra virgin olive oil

Break tips off asparagus. They will break naturally at the appropriate point. Steam asparagus tips until just tender/crisp. Cut off flat ends of grapefruit and set on end. With sharp knife cut away peel with downward strokes. Remove each section with knife carefully to keep them intact. In a bowl combine vinegar and olive oil. Add grapefruit sections and asparagus tips. Toss gently.

Strawberry Rhubarb Parfait

1 cup fresh strawberries
1/4 lb. fresh rhubarb cut in 1/2-inch lengths
1/4 cup sugar
Juice and grated rind of 1 orange
1 cup nonfat yogurt

In saucepan combine all ingredients except yogurt, and bring to a boil over medium heat, stirring to dissolve sugar. Reduce heat, cover, and simmer for about 10 minutes, or until rhubarb is very soft. Chill.

To serve, spoon alternate layers of yogurt and fruit into two balloon goblets, or tall dessert glasses, ending with a spoonful of fruit.

Each one of these dishes combines unusual flavors blending in harmony. A theme favoring the unity created by the essence of love.

The meal may be assembled beforehand to eliminate fuss and bother at serving time. Simple. Elegant.

— CHRISTINE FOX

♊	gemini	May 22- June 21
Mercury		*Mutable Sign of Air*

s	m	т	w	т	ƒ	s
					May 22 *Delay your decision*	23 *Take no risk* Taurus
24 *Lilli Palmer born, 1914*	25 ● Gemini	26 WAXING	27 *Vincent Price born, 1911* Cancer	28	29 Oak Apple Day Leo	30 *Follow your bliss*
31 *Trust a hunch*	June 1 ◑ Virgo	2	3 *Balance returns* Libra	4 Night of the Watchers	5	6 *Count the crows* Scorpio
7 *Walk by the sea*	8 Sagittarius	9 *Draw down the Moon*	10 dyad moon	11 WANING Capricorn	12 *Think clearly*	13 *Trust your heart* Aquarius
14 *Clear the channel*	15 *Learn to forget* Pisces	16	17 ◐ Aries	18 *Shun danger today*	19 Taurus	20 *The Moon is low*
21 SUMMER SOLSTICE Gemini						

Selene and Endymion

It's a simple enough story. But like many another myth, strange aspects prevail, contradictions abound, confusions abide. And that is exactly what gives ancient tales of love their undying charm.

In the cryptic account of the shepherd and the Moon goddess, one of the basic confusions is identity. We have no problem with that of Endymion, a youth of surpassing handsomeness who tended his flocks on Mt. Latmos. But the persona of Selene shifts and shimmers over the millennia during which she was worshipped.

The name derives from *selas*, meaning light or radiance, the early Greek term for the goddess. But she was also known as Phoebe (bright Moon), and in her guise as Hecate she was regarded as a tutelary deity of magicians and sorcerers. In the Hellenistic period the Selene identity fused at times with the goddesses Artemis and Persephone, and the Romans equated her with Diana and Luna.

Some accounts attest that Selene is the daughter of the Sun god Apollo and Theia, Titaness of the Night. Elsewhere she is termed the daughter of the Titan Hyperion and sister of Apollo.

In some versions Selene is a virgin; in others, she has numerous lovers, including Zeus and Pan. But certain of Selene's attributes remain constant. Always she is radiantly beautiful, fluttering bright silver wings, crowned by a crescent-shaped diadem aglow with light. As goddess of the full Moon, she rides across the lunar heavens in a silver chariot drawn by two white horses.

One clear night, Selene looks down and sees Endymion, limbs asprawl, sleeping among his sheep in the mountain forest. Ravished by his beauty, the heart of the goddess catches fire and she seduces him.

What comes next? Two basic versions pop up, equally bizarre. In one, Selene persuades Zeus to grant her beloved one wish. Endymion chooses perpetual youth by means of perpetual sleep, and retires to a deep underground cave. In some mythologies, Selene imposes the same strange narcolepsy on her handsome lover. Whichever, Endymion must have been aroused on occasion, as all sources agree that he fathered fifty daughters with the goddess. And when the full Moon is not visible in the heavens, the ancients believed that Selene was visiting her lover deep in his cavern of repose.

— BARBARA STACY

cancer — June 22- July 23

Moon   *Cardinal Sign of Water*

s	m	т	w	т	ƒ	s
	June 22 *Happiness is inevitable*	23 ● Cancer	24 WAXING Midsummer Day	25	26 *Pearl Buck born, 1892* Leo	27 *Kindle an old flame*
28 *Use your imagination* Virgo	29 *Seek and you will find*	30	July 1 ◐ Libra	2 *Perform a candle spell*	3 Scorpio	4 *Remain flexible*
5 *Divine the future*	6 *A dream comes true* Sagittarius	7	8 *Onward and upward* Capricorn	9 mead moon	10 WANING Aquarius	11 *Mend your fences*
12 *Julius Caesar born, 102 B.C.* Pisces	13	14 *Limit activities*	15 Aries	16 ◑	17 *Keep your distance* Taurus	18
19 Gemini	20 *A red wind blows*	21 *Gather wild herbs* Cancer	22	23 ● Leo	WAXING	

29

The Cat and the Cock

A CAT caught a Cock, and took counsel with himself how he might find a reasonable excuse for eating him. He accused him as being a nuisance to men, by crowing in the night time, and not permitting them to sleep. The Cock defended himself by saying that he did this for the benefit of men, that they might rise betimes for their labours. The Cat replied, "Although you abound in specious apologies, I shall not remain supperless," and he made a meal of him.

> MORAL: The want of a good excuse
> never kept a predator from his prey.

From AESOP'S FABLES, literally translated from the Greek by George Fyler Townsend, London, 1890.

♌	leo	July 24- August 23					
Sun		*Fixed Sign of Fire*					

s	m	τ	w	τ	ƒ	s
					July **24** *Ride the waves*	**25** *Collect fallen feathers* Virgo
26 *Aldous Huxley born, 1894*	**27**	**28** *Jacqueline Onassis born, 1929* Libra	**29** *Surprise an enemy*	**30**	**31** Lughnassad Scorpio	Aug.**1** LAMMAS
2 *Lead the way* Sagittarius	**3**	**4** *Rely only on yourself* Capricorn	**5**	**6** *Dismiss all cares* Aquarius	**7** wort moon	**8** WANING
9 *Time to drift* Pisces	**10** *Patience is a virtue*	**11** Aries	**12** *Honor the goddess*	**13** Diana's Day Taurus	**14**	**15** *Speak your mind* Gemini
16	**17** *Plan your anger* Cancer	**18**	**19** *Wear a mask*	**20** *Take your time* Leo	**21**	**22** WAXING Virgo
23 *Prepare to reap*						

Deirdre's  Destiny

Deirdre of the Sorrows is how the celebrated Irish playwright J. M. Synge referred to her, and this fateful lady—whose destiny has inspired so many Irish writers—takes her place as one of the most tragic figures in literature.

Even before Deirdre was born, the granddaughter of King Conchobhar's harp player, she and those around her faced doom according to the prophecy of Cathbad the Druid. Because of her beauty, Cathbad forecast that "more blood will be shed than was ever shed in Ireland since time and race began. And great heroes and bright candles of the Gael will lose their lives because of her."

In an attempt to avert this disaster, the king ensured that Deirdre's birth would take place in some remote area where she would be raised until of sufficient age for him to marry her. Thus, the makings of a tragedy were already set. Before she returned in maturity to the king, Deirdre fell in love with another man, Naoise, with whom she fled the country, accompanied by his brothers, to escape the king's vengeance.

When the king discovered the whereabouts of the runaways, he sent emissaries to fetch them back, promising safe conduct. However, on their return Naoise and his brothers were treacherously slain, beginning a war in which—true to the prophecy—"great heroes and bright candles of the Gael" lost their lives because of her. Deirdre herself committed suicide after being sent by the triumphant king to live with the man she hated most—the slayer of Naoise.

Deirdre's legend is part of one of the sagas of ancient Irish literature, the *Táin Bó Cuailgne*, which records the exploits of Cúchulainn, sometimes called the Irish Ulysses. The tale has been retold not only by Synge, but by his cofounder of Dublin's Abbey Theatre, William Butler Yeats. It is their colleague Lady Augusta Gregory, however, whose translation of the Táin is regarded as the most authoritative.

"I left out a good deal I thought you would not care about for one reason or another," Lady Gregory says in her introduction to the book, "but I put in nothing of my own that could be helped, only a sentence or so now and again to link the different parts together." And in the course of telling this very feminine story, Lady Gregory couldn't resist making a feminist comment of her own. "Indeed," she wrote, "if there was more respect for Irish things among the learned men that live in the college at Dublin, where so many of these old writings are stored, this work would not have been left to a woman of the house that has to be minding the place and listening to complaints and dividing her share of food."

| virgo | August 24–September 23 |

Mercury — *Mutable Sign of Earth*

s	m	T	w	T	F	s
	Aug. 24 *Recover* *a* *loss* Libra	25	26 *Depend* *on* *foresight*	27 Scorpio	28 *Embrace* *an oak* *tree*	29 Day of Thoth Sagittarius
30 🌓	31 *Consider* *the* *source*	Sept. 1 Capricorn	2 *Bury an* *offering* *in the* *earth*	3 Aquarius	4 *Consult* *the* *tarot*	5 *Jupiter* *is* *bright* Pisces
6 barley moon	7 WANING Aries	8 *Avoid* *a* *quarrel*	9 Taurus	10 *Listen* *to the* *wind*	11 *Stay* *perfectly* *calm* Gemini	12 🌗
13 *Spend* *this day* *alone* Cancer	14 *Agrippa* *born, 1486*	15	16 *Lauren* *Bacall* *born, 1924* Leo	17	18 *Gather* *five* *stones* Virgo	19 *Walk* *until* *weary*
20 🌑	21 WAXING Libra	22 *Dismiss* *all* *doubts*	23 Autumnal Equinox Scorpio			

A Second Wind

When courage fails and all seems lost, a witch ritually summons a second wind, the reserve force that renews hope. The simple act of lighting a candle can be raised to the level of a sacred rite when performed at the right time and in an appropriate atmosphere. Optimism belongs to the mind's domain, the mysterious realm where a change of attitude makes the difference between success and failure, happiness and misery. To lift the spirit is the way to recover normal power and balance.

The first step is the decision to take action. Plan the ceremony and allow enough time for anticipation. Anticipation is an important factor in itself. Challenge the mind with the necessity of choices—where, when, and in what manner—to increase its liveliness. Anxiety and despair deaden human facilities. The mind can become lost in a downward spiral of repetitive thoughts. Determine to banish negativity for one hour.

Choose a quiet, comfortable place where privacy is assured. Within the time of the waxing Moon, from dark to full, sit before a lighted candle with the flame at eye level. Breathe gently as you fix your gaze on the brightest part of the flame. Return to childhood and remember what it was like to play the game of pretend. Make believe the candle flame is something that shines deep within you—call it heart or soul or spirit—a thing unseen yet comprehensible, intangible yet knowable. It is there and it is yours just waiting to be acknowledged and reclaimed. With its image clear in your mind's eye, cup your hand around the flame and softly blow it out.

Hold the memory of its glow as a source of courage whenever you need a refreshing second wind.

s	m	т	w	т	ƒ	s
				Sept. 24 *Find the right words*	25 Sagittarius	26 *Let instinct guide you*
27 *Thoughts are things*	28 Capricorn	29	30 *Open a new door* Aquarius	Oct. 1	2 *Sting born, 1951*	3 *Scorn arrogant criticism* Pisces
4 *Call the corners*	5 blood moon Aries	6 WANING	7 Taurus	8 *Keep your balance*	9 *Two for mirth* Gemini	10 *A brown wind sighs*
11 *Collect oak leaves* Cancer	12	13 Leo	14 *Postpone decision*	15 Virgo	16 *Think thrice*	17 *Know your limits*
18 Libra	19 *Follow the rules*	20	21 WAXING *Carrie Fisher born, 1956* Scorpio	22	23 *Defeat an enemy* Sagittarius	

Hel, Goddess of Death   Johannes Gehrts, 1883

Daughter of Darkness

The Scandinavian goddess Hel made her home beneath the first root of Yggdrasil, the giant ash tree that held the world together. Guarded by her faithful dog, Garmr, Hel ruled the icy-cold underworld of Nifelheim. In early Norse myths all dead souls either spent their afterlife in burial mounds watched over by attendants or joined Hel in her murky domain. Later legends rewarded heroes slain in battle with new life in the glorious halls of Valhalla.

Like the Greek god of the underworld, Hades, whose name and home were the same words, Hel gives us our English word "hell" from an Old Norse root meaning "covered" or "concealed." Hel's world was gloomy, but not a place of torment as penalty for earthly sins. Occasional visits occurred from the fierce wolf, Fenrir, and the serpent, Jormungard, for they were Hel's kin. All three were fathered by Loki, the handsome, sly, and dangerous god whose actions would, an oracle declared, eventually bring the downfall of the gods and victory of chaos as the world ends.

scorpio October 24–November 22

Pluto   *Fixed Sign of Water*

s	m	τ	w	τ	ƒ	s
						Oct. **24** *Summon the white wind*
25 *Daylight Saving Ends 2 AM* Capricorn	**26**	**27** *Face the unknown* Aquarius	**28**	**29**	**30** *Find peace and quiet* Pisces	**31** Samhain Eve
Nov. **1** HALLOW-MAS Aries	**2** *Learn a new song*	**3** Taurus	**4** snow moon	**5** WANING Gemini	**6** *Work and hope*	**7** *A friend is a priceless treasure* Cancer
8 *Take no chances*	**9** Leo	**10**	**11** *Jonathan Winters born, 1925*	**12** Virgo	**13** *Greet a kindred soul*	**14** *Tie the knot* Libra
15 *Relax at twilight*	**16** HECATE NIGHT Scorpio	**17** *Meet at the crossroads*	**18**	**19** WAXING *Honor the elder* Sagittarius	**20**	**21** *Goldie Hawn born, 1945* Capricorn
22						

MARCUS AURELIUS

Emperor of Rome, Stoic philosopher—a rare combination of power and goodness. From his *Meditations*, c. 160 A.D.:

To live happily is an inward power of the soul.

A man does not sin by commission only, but often by omission.

The universe is change; our life is what our thoughts make it.

You will find rest from vain fancies if you perform every act in life as though it were your last.

Never esteem anything as of advantage to you that will make you break your word or lose your self-respect.

Be not careless in deeds, nor confused in words, nor rambling in thought.

It is our peculiar duty to love even those who wrong us.

Nothing happens to anybody which he is not fitted by nature to bear.

Look to the essence of a thing, whether it be a point of doctrine, of practice, or of interpretation.

All is ephemeral—fame and the famous as well.

If you are distressed by anything external, the pain is not due to the thing itself, but to your own estimate of it; and this you have the power to revoke at any moment.

This being of mine, whatever it really is, consists of a little flesh, a little breath, and the part which governs.

Everything is fruit to me that your seasons bring, Nature. All things come of you, have their being in you, and return to you.

Marcus Aurelius, drawn from a statue at Venice by Thomas Hope, London, 1812.

sagittarius November 23-December 21

Jupiter   *Mutable Sign of Fire*

s	m	т	w	т	f	s
	Nov. **23** *Now is the hour*	**24** Aquarius	**25** *Indulge in luxury*	**26** ⬕ Pisces	**27**	**28** *Insist on the best* Aries
29 *Lose not subtance for shadow*	**30** Taurus	Dec. **1** *Pursue an old dream*	**2** *Praise Jove* Gemini	**3** oak moon	**4** WANING	**5** *Wear an amulet* Cancer
6 *Lock your doors*	**7** *Mary, Queen of Scots born, 1542* Leo	**8**	**9** *Beware of crowds* Virgo	**10** ◑	**11** Libra	**12** *A dream comes true*
13	**14** *There is but one of you in all of time* Scorpio	**15** *Comfort a lost soul*	**16** Sagittarius	**17** Saturnalia *Beethoven born, 1770*	**18** ⬤	**19** WAXING Capricorn
20 Eve of Yule	**21** WINTER SOLSTICE Aquarius					

TO MEN ONLY

Eliphas Lévi, the 19th-century French occultist, has influenced generations of those who follow the secret path of high magic. Although his books are serious in tone, dealing as they do with mysteries of the most profound nature, Lévi had a lighter side. Here, from his masterwork *Dogma and Ritual of High Magic*, published in 1856, is a passage displaying the warmth and practical wisdom of the man himself:

"A man who wants to make someone love him (I attribute these deceitful techniques to men only, assuming that women never need them) must first catch the attention and excite the imagination of the person he desires. Let him inspire her with admiration, surprise, horror, or, failing everything else, terror. The indispensable thing is that he stand apart from other men and thus, fix himself, like it or not, in her memories, her apprehensions, her dreams. A Lovelace is certainly not the openly avowed ideal of every Clarissa. But their thoughts dwell on such men in order to reproach them, to curse them, to pity their victims, to wish for their conversion and repentance. Then a secret vanity tells them that it would be a fine thing to be loved by such a man, to love him and yet resist him.

And so Clarissa finds to her surprise that she has fallen for Lovelace; she is angry with herself, blushes, renounces him a thousand times and only loves him a thousand times more. Then, at the critical moment, she forgets to resist him.

"A great disappointment for certain upright women is to find that the man they took for an outlaw, and so became infatuated with, is really a good and virtuous person. The angel then leaves the poor fellow, scornfully remarking that he was not, after all, the devil.

"If you wish to seduce an angel, you must play the part of a devil!...The role of the proper gentleman will seduce no women except those who have no need of it. All the others, without exception, prefer the outlaw type."

The Goat of Mèndes. Lévi's well-known drawing represents the reconciliation of opposites.

♑ capricorn   December 22 - January 20

Saturn   *Cardinal Sign of Earth*

S	M	T	W	T	F	S
		Dec. **22** *Welcome the Sun's return*	**23** Pisces	**24** *Solve a puzzle*	**25** *Humphrey Bogart born, 1899* Aries	**26**
27 *Try harder*	**28** *View life from a hill* Taurus	**29**	**30** *Plan a revel* Gemini	**31** *Ring out wild bells*	Jan. **1** wolf moon 1999 Cancer	**2** WANING
3 *Kindness is rewarded* Leo	**4**	**5** *Diane Keaton born, 1946*	**6** Virgo	**7** *Nature is not precise*	**8** *A loss is a gain* Libra	**9** *Feast of Janus*
10 Scorpio	**11** *No piper pleases all ears*	**12**	**13** *Music eases tension* Sagittarius	**14** *Keep a secret*	**15** Capricorn	**16** *Watch and wait*
17	**18** WAXING Aquarius	**19** *Ours is the magic*	**20** *As above, so below* Pisces			

JANUS

January was named for Janus, the porter or janitor of heaven. He was the guardian deity of gateways, depicted as having two opposite faces, because every door looks two ways. Janus was a concept unknown to the Greeks, but from earliest times one held in high esteem by the Romans, who placed him on almost equal footing with Jupiter. The aid of both gods was invoked prior to every undertaking. To Janus the Romans ascribed the origin of all things: the change of seasons, the ups and downs of fortune, and the civilization of the human race by means of agriculture, arts, and religion. The heads of Janus are crowned with a crescent Moon, the form of the waxing and waning Moons. He holds a key in his left hand to show it is within his power to unlock the future as well as lock away the past. The scepter in his right hand symbolizes his control of the progress of all undertakings. The public worship of Janus was introduced into Rome during the time of Numa Pompilius (715-672 B. C.), but it seems likely that his conception as a deity is as old as the Rome of Romulus.

≋ **aquarius** January 21-February 19

Uranus   *Fixed Sign of Air*

s	m	T	w	T	F	s
				Jan. **21** *Smile witch, laugh, witch*	**22** Aries	**23** *Fortune smiles*
24 ◗ Taurus	**25**	**26** *Dance to a new tune* Gemini	**27**	**28** *There is world enough and time*	**29** Cancer	**30** *Franklin D. Roosevelt born, 1882*
31 ○ *storm moon* Leo	Feb. **1** WANING Oimelc Eve	**2** CANDLE-MAS Virgo	**3** *Discard the useless*	**4** Libra	**5** *Trust a dream*	**6** *Carry a talisman*
7 *Discover a hidden path* Scorpio	**8** ◖	**9** Sagittarius	**10** *Scorn arrogant ignorance*	**11** *Keep your mystery*	**12** Capricorn	**13** *Forgive and forget*
14 Aquarius	**15** *Consider total change*	**16** ● Year of the Hare	**17** WAXING Pisces	**18** *Cybill Shepherd born, 1950*	**19** *Silence is an answer* Aries	

THE ALDER TREE

Fearn—March 18 to April 14

The first three trees of the Celtic Tree Calendar flourish on heights and mountain slopes. By contrast the alder, the fourth, is usually found thriving in thickets beside lakes, streams and rivers. It so favors marshy conditions that the tree seldom grows on drier land. Its black bark scored with cracks and broad oval leaves quickly identify the alder. As the timber dries after felling, its color changes from yellow to orange to red. When dried, the wood is water resistant and does not split when nailed. For centuries alder has provided pilings to serve as building foundations throughout European lowlands.

Charcoal derived from alder wood is superior to all others. Ceremonial magicians are advised to burn their incense on blocks of alder charcoal. The link between alder trees and the element of fire may derive from an early bloom occurring at vernal equinox to welcome spring and the return of the Sun's warmth.

The alder is associated with Bran, a Celtic hero/god. One tale about him is found in the Welsh collection of medieval legends known as *The Mabinogion. The Voyage of Bran to the World Below*, a tale found in Old Irish literature of oral tradition, is another. The sea-god Llyr (Welsh) and Lir (Irish) plays a role in both tales as do black birds: the starling, crow, and raven. The Irish epic describes Bran waking from a dream to find himself in the presence of a goddess and holding in his hand a silver branch of alder. The branch magically springs from his hand to hers once he agrees to set sail for the abode of the goddess.

It is rare to find alder mentioned in European folklore. Old herbals, however, offer many practical uses for alder leaves.

H	pisces	February 20 -March 20

Neptune · *Mutable Sign of Water*

s	m	T	W	T	F	s
						Feb. **20** *Gloria Vanderbilt born, 1925*
21 *Organize your life* Taurus	**22**	**23** Gemini	**24** *Plan a venture*	**25** Cancer	**26** *Perception is strong*	**27** *Stay the course* Leo
28 *Enjoy peace at home*	Mar. **1** *To the pure, all is pure* Virgo	**2** chaste moon	**3** WANING	**4** *Dare to change your mind* Libra	**5**	**6** *Be firm and fair* Scorpio
7 *Head up, shoulders back*	**8**	**9** *Never give up* Sagittarius	**10**	**11** Capricorn	**12** *Jack Kerouac born, 1922*	**13**
14 Aquarius	**15** *Drop a token in a stream*	**16** Pisces	**17**	**18** WAXING Aries	**19** *Summon the green winds*	**20** *Design a new garden* Taurus

45

Rapunzel H. J. Ford, 1889

RAPUNZEL

Once upon a time there lived a man and his wife who for a long time had wished in vain for a child, and at last the woman had reason to believe that heaven would grant her wish. There was a little window at the back of their house, which overlooked a splendid garden full of all manner of beautiful flowers and vegetables. It was, how- ever, surrounded by a high wall, and no one dared to enter it, for it belonged to a sorceress of great power who was feared by everybody.

One day the woman, standing at her window and looking down into the garden, saw there a bed planted with the most beautiful rampion. They looked so fresh and green that she longed to eat them. The desire increased day by day, and because she knew that she could not have any, she pined away and became quite pale and miserable. Then her husband grew alarmed and said, "What ails you, dear wife?"

"Oh," she said, "if I don't get some rampion to eat from the garden behind our house, I shall die." Her husband, who loved her dearly, thought to himself, before you let your wife die you must fetch her some of that rampion, cost what it may. So at twilight he climbed over the wall into the forbidden garden, hastily gathered some rampion leaves and returned with them to his wife. She immediately prepared a salad and ate it with great relish. It tasted so good that the next day her longing for it increased three-fold. If she were to know any peace of mind, there was nothing for it but that her husband should climb over the garden wall again and fetch her some more. So at dusk he returned, but as he climbed over the wall he was terrified to see the witch standing before him. "How dare you," she said as she angrily glared, "climb into my garden and steal my rampion like a thief? You shall suffer the consequences."

"Alas!" he answered, "temper justice with mercy. I am only here by necessity. My wife sees your rampion

46

from our window, and she has such a longing for it that she will die without it." The anger of Mother Gothel, for that was the name by which she was known, cooled a little and she said to him, "If it is as you say, you may take as much rampion as you like, but on one condition only—that you give me the child that your wife is about to bring into this world. All will be well with it, and I will give it a mother's care." The man in his terror agreed to everything she asked. And when the child was born, the enchantress appeared, named the baby Rapunzel, which is the German word for rampion, and took the child away with her.

Rapunzel was the most beautiful child under the sun. When she was twelve years old, the witch shut her up in a tower which stood in a forest. It had neither stairs nor doors, but only high up at the very top a small window. When the witch wanted to get in she stood below and called:

"Rapunzel, Rapunzel,
Let down your hair."

Rapunzel had splendid long hair, as fine as spun gold. When she heard Mother Gothel's voice, she would undo her braids and wind them around a window hook. Then her hair would drop about twenty yards to the ground, and the witch would climb up by it.

After several years it happened that the king's son was riding through the forest and passed by the tower. As he drew near it he heard someone singing so sweetly that he stopped to listen. It was Rapunzel, who in her loneliness passed the time singing to herself. The king's son longed to see the singer, and he sought for the door of the tower but

there was none to find. He rode home, but the song haunted his memory so much that he returned every day to the forest to listen. One day, when he was standing behind a tree, he saw the sorceress coming and heard her call:

"Rapunzel, Rapunzel,
Let down your hair."

Then Rapunzel let down her braids, and the witch climbed up to her. If that is the ladder by which one ascends, he thought, I'll try my luck. And the following day, as darkness fell, he went to the tower and called:

"Rapunzel, Rapunzel,
Let down your hair."

Right away the hair fell down and the prince climbed up it.

At first Rapunzel was terrified, for she had never set eyes on a man before. But the prince spoke to her so kindly, and told her that her song had touched his heart so deeply that he could find no peace of mind till he had

Rampion

seen her. Then Rapunzel lost her fear, and when the prince asked her to marry him she consented at once. She thought, he is young and handsome, and I'll certainly be happier with him than with my old godmother. So she put her hand in his and said, "Yes, I will gladly go with you, only how am I to get down from this tower? Each time you come, bring a skein of silk with you and I will twist it into a ladder, and when it is long enough I will descend by it, and you will take me away on your horse."

They arranged that he should come and see her every evening, for the old enchantress only came in the daytime. The old witch suspected nothing till one day Rapunzel said unthinkingly, "How is it, Mother Gothel, that you are so much harder to pull up than the young prince? He is always with me in a moment."

"Oh, you wicked child," cried the witch. "What are you saying? I thought I had shut you safely away from the whole world, and yet you have deceived me." In her rage she seized Rapunzel's beautiful hair, twisted it twice around her left hand, snatched up a pair of scissors with her right, and snip, snap, cut it off. The beautiful braids lay on the floor. And, worse than this, she was so heartless that she took Rapunzel to a wilderness, and there left her to live in great grief and misery.

In the evening of the day on which she had driven Rapunzel away, the sorceress fastened the braids to the window hook, and when the prince came and called out:

"Rapunzel, Rapunzel,
Let down your hair."

she lowered the hair. The king's son climbed up as usual, but instead of finding his beloved Rapunzel, he found the witch, who glared at him with angry, glittering eyes.

"Aha," she cried mockingly, "you have come to fetch your lady love, but the pretty bird has flown. She sings no more, for the cat has seized her and will scratch your eyes out too. Rapunzel is lost to you. You will never see her again."

The prince was beside himself with grief, and in his despair he leaped from the tower. He escaped with his life, but his eyes were scratched out by the thorns among which he fell. He wandered, blind and miserable, through the forest, eating nothing but roots and berries, and weeping and lamenting over the loss of his lovely bride. So he wandered for several years in misery and happened at last upon the desert place where Rapunzel had been living in great poverty with the twins she had borne—a boy and a girl. He heard a voice which seemed strangely familiar to him and he went toward it, and when he approached, Rapunzel recognized him at once and fell on his neck and wept. Two of her tears fell upon his eyes, and they became quite clear again, and he saw as well as he had ever done. The prince took her to his kingdom, and they lived happily ever after.

presage

by Dikki-Jo Mullen

ARIES 1998 — PISCES 1999

Our ancestral yearning for unity with the celestial, for the spirit of heaven to link with life on Earth, is universal. Ancient ones honored this in creating records of the cosmic drama of planetary patterns. Modern seekers continue to look to the sky for guidance and comfort in understanding life experiences during these times of change.

For hundreds of years, great seers and prophets have predicted that 1998 through the first years of the new millennium will be a cycle of great transformation. There are hints of coming change all around us. Your personal birth sign forecast will guide you during the year ahead so you can make decisions which will assure a bright, successful future in every way. If you were born on the day of a sign change, in astrology known as the cusp, both forecasts will apply.

Check with your personal astrologer, who will use your place and time of birth to ascertain which is your actual Sun sign. The Sun sign is the only part of the horoscope known to most people. It describes your ego, sense of purpose, and identity—how you shine. For more information, study the forecasts for your Moon sign and Ascendant. The Moon will offer insight about domestic and emotional needs, while the Ascendant, or Rising sign, shows how you appear and function as part of the physical world around you.

ASTROLOGICAL KEYS

Signs of the Zodiac
Channels of Expression

ARIES: pioneer, leader, competitor
TAURUS: earthy, stable, practical
GEMINI: dual, lively, versatile
CANCER: protective, traditional
LEO: dramatic, flamboyant, warm
VIRGO: conscientious, analytical
LIBRA: refined, fair, sociable
SCORPIO: intense, secretive, ambitious
SAGITTARIUS: friendly, expansive
CAPRICORN: cautious, materialistic
AQUARIUS: inquisitive, unpredictable
PISCES: responsive, dependent, fanciful

Elements

FIRE: Aries, Leo, Sagittarius
EARTH: Taurus, Virgo, Capricorn
AIR: Gemini, Libra, Aquarius
WATER: Cancer, Scorpio, Pisces

Qualities

CARDINAL	FIXED	MUTABLE
Aries	Taurus	Gemini
Cancer	Leo	Virgo
Libra	Scorpio	Sagittarius
Capricorn	Aquarius	Pisces

CARDINAL signs mark the beginning of each new season — active.
FIXED signs represent the season at its height — steadfast.
MUTABLE signs herald a change of season — variable.

Celestial Bodies
Generating Energy of the Cosmos

Sun: birth sign, ego, identity
Moon: emotions, memories, personality
Mercury: communication, intellect, skills
Venus: love, pleasures, the fine arts
Mars: energy, challenges, sports
Jupiter: expansion, religion, happiness
Saturn: responsibility, maturity, realities
Uranus: originality, science, progress
Neptune: dreams, illusions, inspiration
Pluto: rebirth, renewal, resources

Glossary of Aspects

Conjunction: two planets within the same sign or less than 10 degrees apart, favorable or unfavorable according to the nature of the planets.

Sextile: a pleasant, harmonious aspect occurring when two planets are two signs or 60 degrees apart.

Square: a major negative effect resulting when planets are three signs from one another or 90 degrees apart.

Trine: planets four signs or 120 degrees apart, forming a positive and favorable influence.

Quincunx: a mildly negative aspect produced when planets are five signs or 150 degrees apart.

Opposition: a six sign or 180 degrees separation of planets generating positive or negative forces depending on the planets involved.

The Houses — Twelve Areas of Life

1st house: appearance, image, identity
2nd house: money, possessions, tools
3rd house: communications, siblings
4th house: family, domesticity, security
5th house: romance, creativity, children
6th house: daily routine, service, health
7th house: marriage, partnerships, union
8th house: passion, death, rebirth, soul
9th house: travel, philosophy, education
10th house: fame, achievement, mastery
11th house: goals, friends, high hopes
12th house: sacrifice, solitude, privacy

Ancient astrologers once described eclipses as an attack by a gigantic dragon. This monster in the sky would seem to eat the Sun or Moon, making it disappear. Eventually the luminary would reappear—deposited, it was thought, from the dragon's tail. The Moon's nodes, which correlate with the signs of eclipse activity, were named the head (north node) and tail (south node) of the dragon. North node eclipses are sometimes considered more positive and south node more difficult. Remember, though, that the heavens just generate energy patterns. It's up to us to apply them in productive ways. Eclipses promise excitement; they can herald unusual weather and world events which in turn will impact us as individuals.

There are five eclipses during the year ahead. If one should occur on or near your birthday, be flexible. The status quo is due to change, promising growth.

August 7	Full Moon Lunar with the south node	
August 21	New Moon Solar with the north node	Moon in ascending north node
September 6	Full Moon Lunar with the south node	
January 31	Full Moon Lunar with the north node	Moon in descending south node
February 16	New Moon Solar with the south node	

RETROGRADE MERCURY

Retrograde motion is the backward movement of a planet. Although this is really an optical illusion created by variance in rates of speed of travel between different planets in the solar system as we observe them, we do respond to it. Retrograde cycles bring a need to reconsider, revise, and rest. Planetary energies manifest in unexpected ways. They can be softer or blurred while retrograde. Retrograde motion is not unfavorable, just different.

The most familiar and powerful retrograde cycle is that of Mercury, which occurs 3 to 4 times yearly, lasting about three weeks each time. While Mercury is retrograde, old patterns repeat. People from the past may suddenly reappear. Complete old business, but postpone moves or the signing of contracts. Get extra rest and verify appointments. Travel only to familiar destinations. It is an auspicious time for past life regression and ghost hunting. There will be four retrograde Mercury periods in the coming year.

March 27 – April 20
in Aries
July 30 – August 23
in Leo
November 21 – December 11
in Sagittarius
March 10 – April 3
in Aries and Pisces

ARIES

The year ahead for those born in the sign of the Ram
March 21 to April 20

Ever the pioneer and adventurer, you will be happy to know springtime greets you with action. Volatile Mars, your ruler, moves rapidly through your sign of Aries through the Full Moon on April 11. This influence is like the element fire with which you're so closely associated. Channeled properly, it generates comfort and warmth. If mishandled, you and those nearby could get scorched. You can accomplish a great deal, but control angry impulses with a dash of humor.

Saturn is completing a long two-and-a-half-year passage in Aries. During the past months you've learned about limitations and coping with setbacks. You've become more skilled and stronger, but must resist a touch of cynicism. During June Saturn will touch the Taurus cusp, bringing you a sense of relief and visions of better times ahead.

Mercury is retrograde in Aries from just after the equinox until April 20. It remains in your sign until May 14. This is a marvelous time to refresh and update skills, plan travel, and deepen important communication.

May brings a strong Venus influence. You will attract friendship and admiration. It's easier to enjoy life during May. June accents your 3rd house. A sibling could grow closer. It's easy to get a bit distracted, but ignore cross currents and interference and focus on your true heart's desire.

From Midsummer Day through July 1, Sun and Mercury, then Mars move into Cancer. There may be some conflicts between male and female energies or between home and business concerns. Work through a warlike mood with a bit of compromise. A problem which has been brewing is aired openly. The New Moon in your sister fire sign of Leo on July 23 brings healing and creative solutions.

Life becomes more blissful as planets move through Leo near Lammastide. The eclipses of August 7 and 21 bring new loves and friendships. Your social circle and leisure pursuits are undergoing a catharsis, but the result is positive.

Throughout September health care is in your thoughts. Alternative and natural therapies will work best if you believe in them. Faith is an important factor in any project's success in the weeks before the autumnal equinox.

October illustrates the value of cooperation. Your partnership sector is highlighted. Others have plans and want to involve you. Respect the ideas and motives of coworkers. Be fair. Rules, regulations, and justice are important guidelines to assure harmony in our crowded world.

November opens with Mercury moving into Sagittarius where it will make a favorable trine in your 9th house until just past New Year's Day. The last two months of 1998 bring an eloquence. If you want to write or lecture to groups, proceed with the confidence that you will do well. Involve yourself in learning experiences and travel. Your perspective broadens. It's easy to rise above worries and be optimistic.

Yuletide finds the Sun and Venus square in the 10th house of career. Maintain a low profile at office parties, and keep your own holiday entertaining simple and comfortable. Social situations can be stressful and expensive otherwise. The end of December finds you awash with ambitions and longings. Enjoy what you have—don't let yourself be tormented by thoughts of greener pastures. Make a list of your many accomplishments and love yourself for each one of them.

On January 26 Mars leaves your sector of law and partnership. There will be less competition, less of a need to feel vindicated. The January 31 eclipse affects your 5th house. Relationships with children assume a new dimension, and you will express true love in new ways. Welcome a change of heart as Valentine's Day draws near. A strong accent on the water signs of Pisces and Scorpio early in February makes you rather secretive. Your inner life becomes more active.

The mood shifts February 12 when Jupiter begins a year-long passage through your birth sign. Venus follows, entering Aries on February 21. Your natural effervescence shines. You are gratified as avenues for fulfillment of desires open. Make contacts, and develop plans. There is an overall brightness of outlook until mid-March. Creativity is at a peak. Express the artist within February 21 – March 17 while Venus is conjunct your Sun.

Mars, always so influential for the Aries born, will turn retrograde in your 8th house on March 18. Winter ends with a curiosity about death's mysteries. There can be a message of wisdom and comfort from the spirit realm near the equinox. A sense of déjà vu prevails. Look at repeating patterns to understand the future. As spring begins, give yourself extra rest.

HEALTH

Always exercise your eyes if reading or doing other close work for long periods of time. Take breaks from glaring artificial light during the work day and walk in the full-spectrum daylight. Headaches induced by stress or diet can be a real health concern. Be aware of factors in your lifestyle which bring them on and take precautions. Peppermint tea is a wonderful rejuvenator. Spicy Indian curries or Tex-Mex dishes are diet choices which will enhance health and energy. Saturn is leaving your sign this year. Slowly, your health is improving. The last couple of years have found you fatigued and may have brought other health challenges. You will grow stronger July through August. Dry climates tend to invigorate you.

LOVE

You are attracted by a challenge and will ardently pursue people you admire. However, you may become disenchanted easily and lose interest. You are very visual and will be drawn by the way a romantic prospect looks upon first impression. May and mid-August through early September promise comfort and joy with your nearest and dearest.

FINANCE

You always yearn for the best. Expensive shopping sprees can break your budget. Focus on managing your money this year. Saturn is about to affect your money sector for several years to come, so foresight is a must to assure comfort. Near May Eve a favorable Venus transit enables you to earn a bit of extra income. Investments and other sources of income can materialize during the first half of November.

SPIRITUALITY

Neptune is completing a square to your Sun at the end of November. You will begin a phase of greater spiritual clarity which will uplift you for many years to come. Patience and faith are important until then, as there can be some confusion over what is real and meaningful in a spiritual sense early in the year. Candles, sacred fires, and smudging are all wonderful aids to facilitate meditation and spiritual cleansing. You experience a sense of euphoria while exercising. A mountain hike over sacred ground would be a perfect setting for awakening spiritual feelings. Study the art of very primitive cultures. Prehistoric cave paintings or carvings can be deeply meaningful to you.

TAURUS

The year ahead for those
born in the sign of the Ram
April 21 to May 20

You practical, patient, and industrious Taureans begin the spring season with your ruling planet, Venus, prominent in the 10th house of career. Expect to be highly visible. Your charisma and appearance can directly impact success while this pattern is in force through April 5. There are changes brewing that will affect your profession and aspirations all year. Get the facts straight, and don't panic just because the status quo is threatened. Uncertainty always disrupts you, but have faith that a shift may generate improvement.

Mars moves rapidly through your birth sign from mid-April through late May. It will be easier to exercise, and you may be more active and competitive than usual near your birthday. The Taurus New Moon April 26 will bring the specifics into focus. The week of May Eve is a perfect time to work in the garden. Earth spirits will respond with love to the touch of your famous green thumb. May 29 through Midsummer Day Venus is very strong while transiting Taurus. Your quality of life and overall happiness will peak. It will be one of the best timespans all year for financial and romantic success.

Saturn touches the cusp of your sign on June 9. Before October's end it will bring a hint of important responsibilities needing attention. Approach work cheerfully, and practice good preventative health habits June through October. This will help you bring out the best of a long Saturn transit through Taurus which will begin in earnest the eve of March 1, 1999. Saturn is a friend in disguise, for it rules your sister earth sign of Capricorn. However, this ringed cosmic wanderer does bring reality and practical needs to the fore. Crystals and sacred stones have a special affinity with Saturn. Learn how you can use the wonderful energies they contain for comfort and protection now.

July through August could bring a residential move. You will talk more with family members and acquire a better understanding of their growth and needs. The combination of a Mercury transit through Leo in your 4th house and the summer's eclipse pattern promises this focus on your domestic environment. Be receptive to changing home and family dynamics. It's a perfect time to repair and redecorate your home and surroundings.

September brings new pleasures and loves. Between the eclipse on the 6th and the autumnal equinox, the Sun, Venus, and Mercury in Virgo will move to a trine aspect in your 5th house. Happiness with children and creative breakthroughs are likely. Express affection; tender sentiments will be returned.

After the autumnal equinox your health sector is affected by Libra transits through the third week of October. Be aware of how stress and diet impact wellbeing. Accept imperfections philosophically. A deeper love and appreciation for animals builds. Buy a new bird feeder or adopt a kitten; you'll be amazed at the joy it brings you.

The week before Halloween until November 17 Venus will oppose you. There may be some tensions to resolve with a close associate. If you overcome your famous stubbornness, a satisfactory compromise may develop near the November 3 Full Moon in your sign. That week promises psychic dreams and the awakening of latent gifts.

Mid-November through Yule your 8th house is affected by Mercury. Discuss financial partnerships, and be aware of how others affect your security. Thoughts about the afterlife and spirit world intensify as the days grow shorter. You may acquire a deeper understanding of these mysteries. December 22 – January 3 a favorable mix of Sun and Venus energies makes holiday travel a joy. Seasonal music enhances celebrations then. January 4–25 transits to your 9th house bring a broader viewpoint. Attend a class, discussion group, or look at current publications.

During January and February you will feel the eclipses in your 4th and 10th houses. Choices related to career goals and family life must be made. Be fully aware of inevitable changes developing both at home and work. A Mars opposition can bring some arguments and competition. Don't let a burst of anger become destructive during mid-February. March finds Jupiter, Venus, and, for most of the month, Mercury all cloistered in your 12th house. Seclusion can help you to heal and get centered. You will experience a sense of aloneness. Appreciate the advantages of privacy and cherish the quiet times. Charitable acts and kindnesses you perform warm you with an inner glow as winter ends.

HEALTH
Be sensitive to health messages sent by your body now. You are about to begin a strong Saturn cycle which will bring consequences if you have developed poor health habits in the past. Have a dental check up; your throat, mouth, and teeth tend to be vulnerable. Try rose fragrance in aromatherapy. Be sure to maintain the proper weight. Rosehip herbal tea, which is rich in vitamin C, is a healthy beverage to have regularly. Prepare lightly steamed garden vegetables as a tasty and wholesome snack. October through November is a time when your health takes a turn for the better if you do your part. Sound therapy can work wonders for your overall wellness, but protect your ears from being damaged by loud noises, including music.

LOVE
Your attachments are deep and lasting. Learning to let go of a relationship which has become addictive or outlived its usefulness is a must. Often you will manage the finances when involved in a close relationship. June and September promise happiness from Cupid.

FINANCE
Changes are afoot directly related to your career because of eclipses in August and January affecting your 10th house. Be progressive and flexible. You are a gourmet in every sense of the word and long for creature comforts. Fine clothes and jewelry are hard for you to resist. Purchase only what you can honestly afford this year and all will be well. Accounting, banking, and the study of finance intrigue you.

SPIRITUALITY
A favorable trine aspect from Neptune in Capricorn has been in force since 1984. Meaningful dreams, inspiration from spiritual leaders, and mystical teachings from other lands have all been possible sources of enlightenment for you. The trend ends in January, but you can draw upon spiritual insights you've gained in the past for many years to come. Your special link to Mother Earth and her fruits indicates that plants can draw you closer to the Lord and Lady.

GEMINI

The year ahead for those born in the sign of the Twins
May 22 to June 21

The first days of spring find your ruler, Mercury, marching in a solemn conjunction with Saturn. Cleanliness and efficiency spell success. Assuming the persona best suited to any occasion is second nature to you. With the heavenly Twins as your emblem, there is always a duality within you. March 21–26 is not a time to show the whimsical side. A serious practicality helps you to begin the new year successfully.

Mercury is retrograde March 27 – April 19, underscoring the message of your 11th house and creating a constructive sextile aspect. A second opinion helps solve any problems. Renew professional contacts, and update old applications. A second or third attempt at reaching any goal is likely to work out. Be persistent. Try not to veer away from long-range goals now.

From the end of May through the 4th of July holiday weekend, Mars dashes through your birth sign. You will be powerful and effective. There is new warmth and action which carries you forward. If angry feelings build, examine the consequences before you act. Protect yourself against sunburn near Midsummer Day, and don't go overboard with exercise.

June 24 – July 18 tender and happy forces bless your life with many joys as Venus moves through your sign. Plan a vacation, court a new love, and let artistic expression flourish. Beauty surrounds you. The end of July through mid-August your 2nd house is strong. Balancing financial matters in order to acquire items you need and want will be important. Near Lammas you can go on a shopping expedition. Keep all receipts and compare prices, though. Mercury is retrograde again and you might change your mind.

August's eclipse pattern accents the Aquarius transits of Uranus and Neptune in your 9th house. You may explore new philosophies or be profoundly affected by spiritual awakenings. The trend peaks August 7 at the Full Moon in Aquarius. Faraway places and foreign people turn your thoughts away from the familiar. Daydreams are vivid. September's eclipse squares your Sun and highlights the 10th house. There could be a new authority figure or other challenges affecting your career. Communication is delicate all month. Usually talkative Twins must listen now. Be cautious if speaking or writing about controversial topics. A relative may be cultivating a new social circle. Be understanding and accepting.

Autumn brings first Mercury and the Sun, then Venus to form a trine aspect in your 5th house. From the equinox through October 23, you will be able to combine work with recreation and social life. Friends suggest travels or invite you to share their hobbies and interests. A new romantic involvement delights and surprises you during the colorful, magic-filled weeks of fall. Select traditional autumn colors such as orange, gold, russet, and rich red for your October wardrobe.

The focus is on health from the week before Hallowmas through mid-November. Mars squares you, revealing that stress can play a role in how you feel. Diet is a factor too. Try a seasonal ritual for self-healing and correct any poor habits before Mercury goes retrograde November 21. Postpone Yuletide plans and purchases until after it goes direct on December 11.

The Full Moon in your birth sign on December 3 finds you reviewing the past. Memories are poignant. Focus your attention on the happy times, and enjoy old photos or other keepsakes which make you smile. December 12 through Yule Mercury conjoins Pluto in your relationships sector. A partner expresses new needs and interests; others involve you in their plans. Be cooperative and understanding.

At year's end Saturn changes direction in your 11th house. Discard old dreams and irrelevant goals. Visualize and identify what you want and how you'd like to pursue it. Friends are recovering from difficult times and provide more cheerful companionship near New Year's Eve.

January 1 finds planets in your sister air signs of Libra and Aquarius forming a beneficial grand trine aspect to your Sun. This lucky pattern is in effect through the 25th. Your enthusiasm and energy are high. Studies, travel, and conversation generate agreeable ideas and experiences. Your perpetual zest for the novel and intriguing is fulfilled. January ends as the Leo eclipse falls in your 3rd house. You will be restless. Get both sides of the story if there is disturbing news. Postpone travel until after February 16.

The end of February through March 2 Mercury is elevated, crossing your midheaven. Your visibility is on the rise. It's difficult to keep any secrets at work. If you expend extra effort, a promotion or recognition comes your way. Winter ends with Mercury retrograde in your 10th and 11th houses. You can develop a deeper understanding of ongoing conditions at work or within organizations. Postpone decisions about the future until the spring equinox. Events are unfolding which could change your attitude.

HEALTH

Make it a habit to stretch and tone your arms and legs daily. Maintaining flexibility will benefit your overall health. Your birth sign has a special affinity with the hands. Keep yours well manicured. Protect them with gloves while gardening or exposed to wintry temperatures. Jasmine herb tea and mixed fruit or vegetable salads with fresh bread are healthy diet choices. Try floral bouquet or melon fragrances for aromatherapy. Your health conditions may require extra time to diagnose and might be

karmic or hereditary in origin, as Pluto rules your health house. Retrograde Mercury times can bring temporary weariness. Take care of old maladies and get extra rest when those occur. All year long Pluto will oppose your Sun, source of vitality. Avoid those who are ill— you may be vulnerable to contagious "bugs" or flus. Overall health should be good this year.

LOVE

Humor and variety are elements that will draw you into a love affair. You can be attracted to two prospects at once and have trouble choosing. Short times apart will stimulate your interest and passion as you enjoy sharing new experiences with your beloved to keep the relationship fresh and interesting. July and January promise happiness.

FINANCE

Your security fluctuates. Family members can affect your cash flow. The Moon rules your finances. Always seek additional income and make financial decisions while the Moon is waxing. Be cautious about signing contracts linked to finance when Mercury is retrograde. A Jupiter square in force most of this year can mean high overhead. Don't over-extend or gamble and you should do well. Money matters improve mid-February when Jupiter changes signs. Cultivate an impeccable reputation. You are the center of attention now. Pursue a position of leadership or rise to other new challenges.

SPIRITUALITY

Chants and affirmations are wonderful aids in awakening the spiritual forces within you. Words and language are always important to you. Try celebrating sabbats and esbats with a congenial group or traveling to gatherings of like-minded pagans. With Uranus ruling your 9th house, companionship and mobility are important factors in spiritual growth. Learn more about the Nordic runes in order to acquire a deeper understanding of the cosmic languages which speak to us.

CANCER

The year ahead for those
born in the sign of the Crab
June 22 to July 23

Spring dawns with a powerful alignment of Aries planets stretching across your midheaven in square aspect. With Mars, Saturn, Mercury, and the Sun linked in this pattern, it's important to control your emotions. Always tender and sensitive, the Crab will feel the need to be protected from career stresses and demanding individuals. Remember that it is often your own reactions to a situation which cause pain. Your own mind and heart can create far more problems than others cause for you.

On April 6 Venus joins Jupiter in your sister water sign of Pisces. These two beneficent planets aspect you with a gentle 9th house trine. Suddenly, harmony returns. Your cherished beliefs are supported, and you create success around your most important goals.

Spiritual art and literature draw you closer to the Lord and Lady near May Eve. May finds Mars giving you a renewed sense of confidence and support. It transits Taurus with a harmonious sextile through May 22. The end of the month brings in a 12th house mood. You will be reserved, your childhood shyness revived. Animal friends and nature become a bigger part of your life as summer solstice draws near.

Mercury moves rapidly through your sign June 15–30. Pursue writing; return calls and letters. Travel is successful, especially if you journey to an island, along the shore, or to historical sites. You're more cheerful and will be led to important sources of information, enabling you to find answers to burning questions. The New Moon late on June 23 in your own sign on Midsummer Eve is very magical. Perform a ritual to celebrate your birthday and ask a blessing on goals you want to accomplish during the year ahead.

July is perfect for enjoying water sports; Mars will energize you as it conjoins your Sun in Cancer. You are a determined and influential force. Live in the present, though. Don't expend valuable forces in futile regrets. It's always important for Cancerians to enjoy memories without being haunted by old ghosts. Lammas finds Venus smiling kindly while moving through your birth sign. The good times roll on until August 13. Purchase fashions, plan a party or vacation. A new love is attentive and friends are generous.

The eclipses in August affect your 2nd and 8th houses. They relate strongly to financial matters. Eclipses spell changes. Be aware of how current trends and new conditions can impact earning ability. Resist the temptation to overspend. A relative or business associate could affect your financial situation.

September brings Virgo planets in a supportive sextile in your 3rd house. You will acquire valuable information. Phone calls, letters, and conversations are most revealing during the three weeks before autumnal equinox. It's a marvelous time to work with computers and other modern technologies. September 24 – October 10 Mercury in your 4th house centers your thoughts on home and family life. A real estate transaction or family festivity may be part of this.

On October 11 Neptune completes a long retrograde in Capricorn, the sign opposing you. It has created a tendency to be a bit too trusting of others in past years. Good or bad, associates often have not been as you perceived. Dubious advice or lack of support for your plans could have been a problem. This trend is fading away completely by the end of November.

October 24 – November 16 Venus makes a romantic trine in your 5th house.

Your decorations and costume for Samhain will be especially artistic. Try baking some elaborate holiday goodies to welcome in the Witches' New Year on October 31. A friend will be charmed. As November progresses, health may need a bit of attention. Wrap up warmly against autumn's chill and get enough rest. Mercury transits your 6th house of health November 1 – January 6. Learn all you can about wellness. It's a perfect time to experiment with natural remedies and to use the power of positive thinking to enhance strength. Relationships of all types are entering a more wholesome phase near Yule.

1999 opens with a Full Moon in Cancer on January 1. Since the Moon is your ruler, this brings a sense of vision and promise to the future. Take time to set out a tarot card reading, rune cast, or other favorite divination. The four weeks following this special lunation provide you opportunities for growth and improvement in every way.

During February planets in Scorpio and Pisces form a grand trine in water signs in your birth chart. Health improves, and you accomplish a great deal. Act on a creative inspiration. Visit the theater or take in a concert or art exhibit near Valentine's Day while Venus is especially strong. Late winter isn't the best time for travel. Since you are quite domestic, you can find plenty to keep you content around your own home.

March opens with Saturn moving into Taurus. Over the next two years, this brings substance to long-range plans. Goals are more reachable and clearly defined. The company of the very old and the very young cheers and comforts you. Friendship spans the generation gap gracefully.

HEALTH

Your digestion is delicate. Never eat when upset. Use care with unfamiliar cuisine, especially if it is very rich and seasoned. Papaya enzyme can soothe the stomach. Cinnamon tea will warm and cheer you. Try wintergreen for aromatherapy. Soups and dairy dishes are wonderful menu choices. Jupiter rules your health sector, indicating longevity and the ability to recover from illness. Through mid-February Jupiter will be in Pisces at a trine to your Sun. This promises good health. Being near the ocean or lakefront does wonders for your well-being. Your emblem, the Crab, exemplifies this tie with water.

LOVE

A partner must be compatible with your relatives, especially your mother, to make you content with a relationship. Your generosity and sensitivity make you a delightful companion if you can overcome memories of old, lost loves. The last few years have been difficult for love because elusive Neptune has been in your 7th house. It finally moves on this year, and romantic prospects are improving. Late October through November and the month of February promise bliss.

FINANCE

Your birth sign is shared with more bankers and millionaires than any other. Usually you are well paid and manage money wisely. This year can bring some upheaval, though. Four of the five eclipses fall in your 2nd and 8th houses, relating to money matters. Be flexible, and don't invest in risky ventures. Take advice with the proverbial grain of salt. Carry a jade charm or lucky coin for financial protection. Practice being patient.

SPIRITUALITY

The ocean always makes you aware of the presence of divine forces. If you can't visit the coast, purchase tapes and art work featuring sounds and sights of the sea. Meditate on the various water deities from Neptune to mermaids and undines. Mother goddess and Moon goddess teachings are also very meaningful to you. Reflect on them, collect images of them for your altar. The Moon is your spiritual symbol. Honor the lunar phases. Bask in her glow and spiritual awareness will awaken. The Full Moon on January 1 ushers in a deeply spiritual month.

LEO

The year ahead for those
born in the sign of the Lion
July 24 to August 23

Spring surrounds you with warmth and success. The Sun and four planets are in your sister fire signs of Aries and Sagittarius. Through the middle of April, Mars makes it easy for you to promote beliefs and causes which are meaningful to you. Team spirit is strong, and you can enlist the help of associates in realizing goals through Beltane holiday.

Mercury is making a long, favorable passage through your travel sector. Late March through May 13 you can benefit from exploring. Return to favorite old haunts until April 20 while Mercury is retrograde. After that, strike out into new territory. That's the start of an especially good time for foreign travel or for learning another language.

Mid-May through summer solstice there is much activity in your 10th house. You will make plans regarding your career and could revamp an existing job or seek a new one. Early June favors gardening. Saturn squares your Sun from June 9 until late October. This is a background influence operative throughout that time. It underscores ambition and the need for accomplishment. Much will be expected of you. Steady effort and patience eventually lead to success; don't rely on quick solutions. On June 30 Mercury enters your sign of Leo. Your natural acting ability and flamboyance will be expressed in your conversations and letters during the nine weeks ahead. Don't adhere too closely to old habits and ideas during July and August. New information may bring a different viewpoint to the fore. Business travel will be productive during July and again the first week of September.

Near your birthday, exciting changes are afoot. August brings a solar eclipse in Leo. Since the Sun is your ruler, this is especially potent. Don't resist the new order coming into your life. A different job, relationship, or home may be in the stars soon. The long-term picture will be brighter than it might seem at first glance. Venus enters Leo on August 13. Romantic, loving, and generous, this transit promises you more happiness by the autumnal equinox.

Music and color bring pleasure as summer wanes. Select a new picture or art object for your office. Plan a picnic near your birthday to honor the summer's bounty. A solar amulet or clothing in the sunset colors should be worn for healing and protection.

September accents your 2nd house. Financial planning will be in your thoughts. Conversations revolve around work, spending power, and earning potential. Take advantage of new options or follow through on a suggestion made by a loved one. Mars is in your sign all month long. You're highly motivated and can accomplish a lot if you're not overcome by anger and impatience. Allow plenty of time for commuter travel so that a traffic snarl doesn't delay you, causing stress or even road rage. Use humor to cope with forceful people during September.

October 1–10 Mercury, Venus, and the Sun transiting Libra make a favorable sextile aspect in your 3rd house. This is a perfect time for selling and promotion, as well as study, negotiation, and travel. As Samhain approaches, Saturn retrogrades back from Taurus into Aries, where it will remain for several months. This brings greater kindness from influential people and smooths over age gap differences. Coping with responsibilities becomes second nature.

A square from Venus October 24 – November 16 promises a new twist regarding your social life. A party might not be what you expected; a loved one may be unpredictable. Be very considerate and correct in all dealings with others. You are naturally gregarious and are often accused of being the zodiac's party animal. Keep this in check from late October to mid-November. Select a moderate, healthy diet; and don't celebrate with money earmarked for bills.

Mid-November through December Sagittarius transits heal and support you. It's easier to make the right choices. Communication with those you care for improves. The Full Moon on December 3 illuminates your 11th house. A vision of the future comes through dreams or meditation. Kind friends from the past are in touch before Yule. December 11 – January 4 favors adopting an animal friend or otherwise becoming involved with wild creatures. Volunteer at the local animal shelter, feed wildlife, or honor your familiar in solstice celebrations.

January brings another eclipse in your sign; this one is lunar. It occurs the 31st, but you will sense its promise all month long. Conditions around you are changing, and emotions are strong—adapt, explore. Upkeep of your surroundings and attention to health are musts. Candlemas ushers in a strong Mars aspect which will last through the equinox. Be patient with relatives; make your home peaceful and safe. Exercise moderation if involved in winter sports such as skiing. February 23 – March 15 Venus is favorable. Kindness is expressed by those who share your spiritual beliefs. Enjoy imported foods, clothing, or music. Travel before March 8, then stay close to home until winter's end.

HEALTH
Cardiovascular exercise is always important as your birth sign is closely identified with the heart. Leos are prone to backaches; but massage, chiropractic care, and warm baths can offer relief. Your emblem, the Lion, sleeps up to twenty hours each day. Like the big cats, you might require extra sleep and tend to be nocturnal. A schedule which allows you to sleep late and work in the evening would make optimum use of your energy. Chamomile herb tea and plenty of fresh citrus fruits are healthy menu choices. Island cooking, featuring dishes from Hawaii (a Leo state) and the Caribbean, is also good. Try lemon and carnation in aromatherapy. A favorable trine from Saturn in Aries indicates health will be best March through May and November through January.

LOVE
Your pride and confidence make you feel surprised by rejection. Although you are deeply affectionate and will take a disappointment in love with difficulty, your dignity carries you through. You will seldom pursue an old flame again. It has been said that one only knows what it is to be truly loved after being loved by a Leo. Children are especially precious to you. The eclipse pattern this year warns against hasty decisions about commitment—also, relationships may be changing. A long-term bond may loosen. April, May, and late November through mid-December favor love.

FINANCE
There is something of the gambler in you. Don't let risks or false optimism get you into difficulty. A hobby or your creative gifts can generate extra income. The entertainment, tourism, and recreation industries are profitable. The best financial cycle of the year begins in February when Jupiter enters Aries for a year-long transit. It will usher in opportunity, reward, and a better standard of living.

SPIRITUALITY
Holiday pageants, seasonal festivals, and celebrations make it easier for you to sense the divine. Instinctively you know that the gods and goddesses don't want us to take life seriously, but rather to live and enjoy it. Art, literature, and theater with a spiritual theme will uplift you too. Explore sun god archetypes. Use images of them on your altar. Magic from sunny, tropical islands or jungles will evoke spiritual awareness.

VIRGO

The year ahead for those
born in the sign of the Virgin
August 24 to September 23

A reputation as the zodiac's worrier and worker often makes Virgos complain that their birth sign isn't too exciting. Spring until mid-October brings you the opportunity to display just how warm and talented you really are. The north node of the Moon is making a rare, once-in-nineteen-years passage through your birth sign. This helps you to develop latent talents, be noticed by influential people, and broaden your scope of activity. Accept all invitations and express a zest for life.

Spring begins with your 8th house accented. Through March 26 you may sense a connection with the afterlife and astral world. A friendly greeting from a loved one who has passed over or a blessing from an angelic guardian greets you with the new season. Money may be tied up in investments or earmarked for bills. Good or bad, financial matters aren't quite as they seem.

Mercury turns retrograde March 27 through the first three weeks of April. Mercury is your planetary ruler, and this regular cycle occurring several times yearly really affects you. Verify appointments and use care in making promises. Reflect, take time to rest, and all will be well. The end of April until May 23 a favorable Mars trine helps you create good fortune with positive actions and confidence. You accomplish much and are an inspiration to others. It's a marvelous time for travel, especially if you plan to visit a health spa or retreat center.

The end of May through Midsummer Day Venus in your sister earth sign of Taurus improves financial matters. Your spiritual connection with the land deepens. Tour an interesting cave, visit a garden or national park. Answers to a dilemma may come as a result of the centered feeling this will generate.

The long, bright days of summer highlight your midheaven. Your ambitions and expectations about work are high, and a competitive spirit builds. Be patient and thoughtful. Eventually your value will be more widely recognized. Your aspirations undergo a transformation by Lammas Eve. August accents your 12th house with Leo transits, including retrograde Mercury. Background research and testing of techniques lead to success. Develop depth of concentration. Being alone will seem more enjoyable.

September opens with an eclipse brewing in Pisces, aspecting you by opposition. Partners and associates are going through a catharsis. Don't take it personally if a familiar group breaks up. Let others grow and change. From September 7 through autumnal equinox Mercury and Venus dance together through your own sign of Virgo. You will charm and attract others. Cultivate new social and business contacts. It's an optimum time for travel and study.

October brings Mars out from its subtle, hidden position in your 12th house into your own birth sign where it will remain through Thanksgiving Day. There is a need to act and to meet challenges. You are motivated and enthused. Keep a perspective, and don't push yourself too hard in fitness programs or sports. Controversy surrounds you. Make constructive efforts at improvement, but use care if too much anger is building within or around you.

Late November through December 11 a retrograde Mercury spins through your 4th house. Repairs and cleaning around your home may require attention. Be patient with less than perfect family situations; problems will smooth over close to Yule. Mid-December brings many invitations. The bright social cycle continues through January 3, generated by a well-aspected Venus in your 5th house of pleasure. A loved one would treasure a holiday treat or unusual gift you created. Artistic skill peaks now.

January favors travel. Mercury is the celestial courier in mythology. As children of Mercury, Virgos are frequently enthused about exploring new places and learning other languages. The first three weeks of the new year allow you to indulge this preference or to make plans for a future odyssey. At Candlemas Mars moves into a sextile aspect in your 3rd house. You will express yourself effectively. It's easy to absorb new studies. Pursue teaching or speaking opportunities during February. The March 2 Full Moon in your sign will heighten your intuition and new possibilities will appear.

The last days of winter find Mercury turning retrograde again. Your 7th and 8th houses are affected. Be tolerant and patient with partners. Relationships are in a state of flux. Postpone decisions about financial matters until April 3.

HEALTH

Health is a favorite topic for Virgos, but be careful of over-treating any maladies or mixing different medicines. Stress and psychosomatic ills may create health problems. You are sensitive to food additives and will fare best on a natural diet. High fiber foods can help regulate your often delicate digestive tract. Apples, cranberries, peaches, dill, and raspberry leaf herb tea will tend to heal and strengthen you. Aromatherapy with lavender is wonderful for you. The eclipse pattern this year affects your 6th, 7th, and 12th houses. This can impact health conditions in the lives of those near you. Try to avoid contact with those who suffer from a contagious illness. If caring for those who are sick, take frequent breaks so the stress doesn't wear you down. In March Saturn moves forward to trine your Sun over a several-year period. This will mark a time of healing and increasing strength. The past two years or so

health has probably needed some extra attention, but better times are ahead from late 1999 on. A clean, orderly environment adds to your well-being.

LOVE

You offer constructive criticism to those you love. Be sure to balance this with words of praise and encouragement. A working or learning environment can generate romance. You like sharing worthwhile projects with those you care about. Virgos are often happiest with each other or with a Taurus mate. September and the Yuletide season are the most favorable times to make a love connection.

FINANCE

As an earth sign, you are concerned about security. A job with an attractive benefits package will appeal to you and relieve worries about the future; however, you're emotionally very tied to your work and will want a job you can believe in too. You like to analyze financial situations and learn more about your profession to step up your earning power. Friendships with coworkers can lead to new financial opportunities. Old debts or responsibilities may draw on your resources now. Your long-range financial picture, about two years in the future, is more promising than the present. The months of June, September, and October are best for money matters.

SPIRITUALITY

Your emblem, the Virgin, reveals that the Maiden and other Virgin Mother archetypes can be deeply meaningful. Healing miracles will affect you. Learn all you can about various spiritual healing techniques. Visits to sacred wells and other places known to evoke healing can heighten spirituality in your life. Since you relate to words, detailed organization, and greenery, the Celtic Tree Alphabet is an ideal vehicle to stimulate spiritual understanding. Rune stones and the lore of healing herbs are also suitable. The New Moon in your sign on September 20 brings a spiritual focus.

LIBRA

*The year ahead for those
born in the sign of the Scales*
September 24 to October 23

Being born under the sign of marriage and partnership, relationships are always dear to your heart. Springtime begins with Aries planets grouped in your 7th house, the sector of law and partners; you will become even more focused on helping those you love. The long-term implications of commitments will be in your thoughts until June 8 when Saturn changes signs.

The expectations of others and plans they make involving you may lead to some stress through April 12 due to a strong Mars opposition. This will peak at the Full Moon in your sign of April 11. The art of compromise is second nature to you, so employ it to smooth away tensions. By May Eve negotiations are in progress.

Listen carefully and use caution in making promises through May 15. At the end of May, your energy level picks up. Enjoy exercise and sports as midsummer approaches.

During the first half of June, a trine from Mercury lets others see your point of view. Humor and goodwill brighten intimate ties. Venus, your ruler, enters your sister air sign of Gemini just after the summer solstice. Creative ideas, spiritual art or music, and travel bring pleasure through mid-July. Befriend those from another land or spiritual background, and new friendships may warm your summer.

The eclipses in August accent the needs of children. New aspirations develop, and old goals no longer appeal. Romantic involvements are in a state of flux; adopt a wait-and-see attitude just after Lammas. Resist involvement with new organizations until you learn more about the other members.

September finds your 12th house highlighted first by the Sun, then Mercury and Venus. Others find it hard to relate to your inner fantasy life. Communicate about important issues, but don't try to convert others to your way of thinking until after the autumnal equinox. Dreams have interesting symbolism regarding your own needs, but don't interpret them literally in September. Keep a positive state of mind in the weeks before the autumnal equinox. You can create your own bliss or misery with the power of thought.

On September 24 Mercury enters your own sign of Libra and aspects Mars favorably. A good cycle for calls, letters, and short journeys begins now and lasts through the first week of October.

Your beauty and charm are in evidence from the beginning of October until just before Samhain. Venus, your ruler, will create benign forces as it moves through your sign of Libra. Opportunities arise which may open doors to a better life—pursue them. Both finances and love take a turn for the better near your birthday.

All Hallow's Week ushers in a more practical cycle. Your 2nd house is strong. You will seek stability and security. November brings extra commuter travel and a restlessness, due to a Mercury sextile which is in force the month long. Current events will intrigue you. A favorable Venus aspect November 17 – December 10 allows you to work on sensitive points and find solutions.

Mars enters your sign and moves toward a conjunction with your Sun November 27 – January 25. Yuletide finds you active and assertive. Don't let confrontations develop, and be patient with holiday crowds or traffic. Stress can be high, so take time to relax. Exercise provides a healthy release. Your competitive spirit awakens, and you will play to win. You will enjoy relaxing and entertaining at home from December 11 through Yuletide when Venus transits your home and family sector. The end of 1998 finds Saturn retrograding back into an opposition with your Sun. Others need a lot from you now, and you may tend to worry about a partner.

On January 4 Venus moves into Aquarius where it will move toward a conjunction with Neptune and Uranus in your 5th house by the month's end. Romantic interludes have a surprise and fated quality. If lonely, you could connect with a true soul mate. Spiritual forces inspire creative expression. If you pursue your favorite art form with enthusiasm, you'll be rewarded with exceptional results.

The eclipses of January 31 and February 16 affect your 5th and 11th houses. Interest in old hobbies and group affiliations dwindles. A change of heart on many levels is in progress near Candlemas. The first week of February favors travel and stimulating new studies. Valentine's Day weekend Jupiter begins a beneficial yearlong passage through your 7th house. The health and wealth of those you are closest to will improve. Partnerships are entering a more nurturing phase for you as the spring equinox nears.

A Venus opposition moves into aspect February 22 – March 17. Your generosity and support brighten the lives of others, but don't go to extremes and let charity outweigh compensation. Winter ends with Mercury retrograding in your 6th house of health. Protect yourself from chills and eat fresh, healthy foods. Examine and eliminate sources of stress.

HEALTH

Your birth sign has a special association with the kidneys. Cranberry juice, vitamin C supplements, and enough water should help keep them flushed of poisons or infections. Strengthen your lower back with daily stretching and other exercises—it's another vulnerable area. You often crave sweets, but enjoy them in moderation. Consider fruit, honey, and frozen yogurt instead of rich desserts. Health philosophies from the East such as acupuncture or ayurvedic practices help many Librans. Select Asian cuisine, figs, green beans, corn, peas, and green tea for your menu. Promote healing with coconut or patchouli scents. Your health might have been affected by the demands of someone close to you or by contagious illnesses over the past several years. That trend is ebbing as Jupiter and Saturn change signs. A healthier, stronger cycle is starting by the year's end.

LOVE

Both Uranus and Neptune are in your 5th house of love, making a beneficial trine beginning in November. Love trends are definitely improving. You will be liberated from old heartaches or disappointments. A spiritual connection with a special love may form. Existing relationships transform for the better. You dislike and almost fear being alone. A balanced relationship is always an important priority for Libra, the zodiac's ultra-romantic.

FINANCES

Your artistic skills can generate income. Law and social sciences are other fields you may find worthwhile and lucrative. With the Scale of Justice as your emblem, you will be very ethical in business practices. The autumn season finds favorable influences in your money sector. Avoid arguments or excessive stress connected to money after January 26. Mars enters your 2nd house then and remains through the end of winter.

SPIRITUALITY

Libra has a special affinity with the cultural traditions of China, Japan, and India. Quotations from holy books, pictures, and statues of god/goddess archetypes from those countries will be rich in meaning for you. Yoga would add to your spiritual awakening. The mysticism attached to martial arts, *feng shui*, and the I-Ching are also worthwhile paths to explore. Always make your surroundings beautiful. Lovely objects and harmonious colors will help you recognize the forms and faces of the Lord and Lady all around you.

SCORPIO

*The year ahead for those
born in the sign of the Scorpion*
October 24 to November 22

Expect subtle power plays to unfold regarding money and possessions as the vernal equinox approaches. Pluto, your celestial ruler, has just begun a long retrograde cycle. Until this culminates in mid-August, you will experience changing values and priorities. Analyze patterns in order to unlock the secret of financial success. A job skill you learned in the past may suddenly be in demand again.

Family life and your home assume a subtle glamour as Neptune begins a passage through your 4th house. Ever the detective, you will be fascinated by secrets about your heritage and will discover new qualities in loved ones. A relative who has been out of touch might suddenly reappear. A friendly ghost can haunt a stairway or seldom-used room.

Real estate transactions may be confusing. Humor and patience will speed success. You will grow through involvement with organizations. The Moon's north node makes a stimulating sextile aspect from your 11th house until October. Reach out to new groups, and rise to the occasion if called upon to fill a leadership role. Coven members might decide to support political issues or other worthy causes. As a result, you will develop a deep respect for the kind of strength wielded by numbers.

You will abandon your usual cloak of privacy and reserve to become more proactive by May 11's Full Moon in your own sign of Scorpio. Record your dreams that week. They can be rich in clues regarding new potentials and opportunities.

The summer solstice is strongly flavored by Saturn. It will be entering Taurus in June, creating dynamic aspects in fixed signs. These promise changes in closest partnerships by summer's end. Allow loved ones the freedom to discover their own destinies. It isn't the time to give in to the legendary jealousy or possessiveness which can be Scorpio's undoing. An upbeat trine from Mars rescues you after July 7 when it enters your sister water sign of Cancer. This ushers in a cycle when you rise above petty limitations and direct your efforts toward worthwhile concerns.

Water sprites and mermaids beckon you through Lammastide. Cancer transits compliment Jupiter in Pisces, surrounding you with friendly water sign influences. Explore the many roles water plays in your life. Its spiritual symbolism, health benefits, travel and career related opportunities will literally flood you. August brings an exciting if abrupt change with eclipses jolting your home and career sectors.

Your natural dignity and self-control help you to gracefully balance domestic life with your professional persona. There are important synchronicities unfolding. Your timely response will turn any negative attention into positive recognition. Let go of the status quo; the cosmos are discouraging your usual purposeful intensity. Your unselfish desire to regenerate, to make a difference for the better, can be expressed as you establish improvements in home life. Your home is usually overflowing with keepsakes. Each tells a story. As the summer ends, organize and display your treasures free of clutter. Clear away the debris which can too often hamper your forward progress.

Autumn finds your storytelling ability and flair for debate in top form. Any who have offended you will be defeated by your subtle methods of retaliation as Hallowmas nears. Resist the temptation to verbally and mentally shred those who have been an annoyance. Instead, direct your reserves of mental strength constructively. You could develop latent ability as a spiritual healer. Write that mystery novel you've been composing in your head, or plan a pilgrimage to a sacred site.

The reputation for passion linked to your sign will be in evidence during November. Jupiter will turn direct in your 5th house, the love sector, while Venus moves rapidly through Scorpio. Your yearning for depth and intimacy with your nearest and dearest may manifest by Thanksgiving. For an even more intense bond, try exploring early childhood memories, dreams, or past life insights with your beloved.

The Yuletide season finds your co-ruler, Mars, in the midst of a transit through your 12th house. This spans the first weeks of the new year as well. Your perpetually active inner life will become more colorful and vivid, while you will shun fanfare outwardly. It might surprise you if friends and relatives born under air signs accuse you of withholding information. You will manage to satiate their curiosity and still be discreet with really important matters. Your natural desire not to be too open and vulnerable is accented during the short, dark days of the year.

Expect an abrupt change as Mars begins a long passage through Scorpio on January 27. It will be your guiding force through the spring equinox and beyond. Your great passions for everything from love to work to social concerns will be expressed dramatically. Your capacity for effective action can astound and amaze. The winter months are about the proper use of this power. You will be driven to explore new planes of expression. To achieve this, try meditating on a soaring eagle, noble wolf, or jeweled dragon.

HEALTH

The reproductive organs and elimination system can often be the origin and focus of health concerns. Saturn, the planetary indicator of health, will leave your 6th house in early June. You will enjoy more energy and better vitality than you have had for several years. From the end of October until March 1, it will hover again on the cusp of your health house. An old condition might need monitoring; be gentle with planning fitness programs and lean toward simple, small meals. Healing will progress and strength improves as the winter ends. Horehound candy or herbal tea can be a great overall tonic. Try using the scent of pine to stimulate confidence and strength.

LOVE

With Jupiter, planet of growth and blessings, in your 5th house of pleasure until mid-February of 1999, expect a memorable year for romance. An ocean voyage or pursuit of common goals can be the catalyst for deeper involvement. Venus augments this promise of an important love connection April 7 – May 3, July 20 – August 12, and October 25 – November 17, 1998 as well as January 29 – February 20, 1999.

FINANCE

Your financial sector, the 2nd house, is affected by Pluto. You will begin to see wealth in different terms. New values emerge. The answers to financial problems can be found between November 1, 1998 and January 6, 1999 when Mercury's influence joins Pluto.

SPIRITUALITY

Understanding the afterlife and reincarnation will always be important in your spiritual quest. Scorpio has a special tie to the mysteries surrounding birth and death. Study the Greek myth of Hades and Persephone for more insight. The weeks of the Full and New Moons in Scorpio on May 11 and November 18 can bring with them spiritual awakening.

SAGITTARIUS

The year ahead for those
born in the sign of the Archer
November 23 to December 21

Springtime greets you with applause and appreciation. Your ruling planet, Jupiter, is exalted by house position in your birth chart throughout 1998 while at a square to your Sun. Your image and reputation take on new polish. There is a hint of myth and legend, a larger than life quality, around you. Enjoy meetings, public functions, and the wider parameters of activity; but keep a sense of balance and perspective. Don't neglect details, do keep promises.

Mars trines you through April 13, highlighting the 5th house. The early spring is the perfect time to begin an exercise program or channel creative effort into a new hobby. A powerful group of transits in the fire signs lends new potency to your element. Meditation and ritual honoring fire elementals and deities promise unusual rewards from Eostre (Christian Easter) until May Eve.

Your love for and rapport with animals is illustrated by the melding of the horse with human in your cosmic emblem, the Centaur. May 1 through Midsummer Eve your 6th house, which relates especially to small or domesticated animals, is brightened by first the Sun and Mars, then by Venus. Animal friends can benefit from your care and companionship more than ever. You could win a prize if entering one of them in a competition. Animal-oriented organizations can help you to link up with important new friends as well. The Full Moon in your sign on June 10 lights the deeper significance of this pattern.

The week of that lunation brings spiritual awakening through examining other religions and philosophies. You may be inspired to begin a new study. Through the solstice you will feel motivated. The competitive spirit others recognize in you so often will be in full flower. You will make every effort to be a winner and have an excellent chance of doing so.

July through September you will begin to feel Saturn's entry into your health sector. Get enough rest and eat light, healthy meals through the heat of summertime. Develop health and fitness goals to carry into the new millennium.

August's eclipses excite your 3rd and 9th houses. Travel plans become important, but are subject to change. Do background research if making an unusual or unfamiliar journey. You can learn a great deal at this time; old concepts are changing. Memories of a grandparent or childhood companion can be vivid and meaningful near Lammastide. You enjoy learning and are something of a perpetual student. The late summer may bring some frustration regarding educational plans. Be patient and receptive to changes. Temporarily, at least, it might be best to abandon formal education for self-teaching or a vocational program.

October begins with Venus entering your 11th house and gliding into a harmonious sextile aspect. Effort expended in relationships will meet with a friendly response. Your social circle widens through the 24th. A new friend offers valuable suggestions and opportunities. During the week before All Hallow's Eve you will suddenly enjoy being alone more than usual. Scorpio planets in your 12th house bring a need for peace and privacy. A dream or meditation session helps you to become your own best friend and to accept experiences from the past philosophically.

On November 1 Mercury begins a long passage through your own sign, conjoining your Sun through January 6. This is a marvelous cycle for travel and for pursuing studies. Your eloquence allows you to resolve old misunderstandings. Speaking and writing are truly inspired just before and after Yule. Often you have been accused of being tactless, but you will be able to lose that foot-in-mouth reputation forever as 1999 begins. If you have wanted to write for publication, now is the time to make the dream a reality.

Planetary activity in your 2nd and 3rd houses in January encourages you to examine what material possessions and wealth really mean. There may be an urge to acquire new belongings and to discard those that are outdated or superfluous. Treasure and appreciate what truly matters and let go of the rest. An unusual person may be visible in your neighborhood. Good or bad neighbors aren't quite as they appear. The eclipse on January 31 brings specifics to light. You will have an opportunity to re-evaluate the accuracy of your first impressions and satisfy the need to get both sides of every story.

Candlemas through February 20 Venus squares your Sun and moves through the home and family sector. Balance sentiment and affection with humor and regard for the individual growth and goals of loved ones. It's easy to be a little too protective and generous now. Add music or a new piece of art to your home.

Jupiter enters your fellow fire sign of Aries as winter ends. New opportunity for a child makes you happy. Your creative potential is about to unfold. March is a good time to indulge in a bit of risk taking or competition.

of how age and climate affect your health. Try lemon balm herb tea for energy and rejuvenation. Use clove oil or crushed cloves as aromatherapy for strength and optimism. April and November through January should bring good news about health. Italian cuisine has a special link to your birth sign. Include its rich variety in your menus this year.

LOVE

Over the past couple of years the influences of Saturn and eclipses have brought some trying times. Romance has been tinged with responsibility or old regrets. The last remnants of that pattern are passing after Candlemas. Jupiter enters your 5th house of love February 12, 1999 for a year-long stay. Cupid will smile on one of the happiest years you have ever known beginning then. Venus will shine in your birth sign from mid-November through mid-December. Purchase new finery for Yule, and reach out to those you admire then. The weeks of June 9 and October 5 bring Full Moon cycles which show potential for attracting love and happiness.

FINANCE

Retrograde Pluto in your sign until early August shows you re-evaluating investment strategies or tax and insurance payments. Be aware of how budgeting and habits are affecting your security. Past choices and how they have created the present financial situation are in your thoughts. Near your birthday you will feel more optimistic. Pursue opportunities just after the New Moon January 17. That lunation triggers positive action in your 2nd house, ruling cash flow.

HEALTH

The lower back, upper part of the thighs, and blood pressure or blood sugar levels may be the focus of health concerns. Saturn, the celestial taskmaster, hovers on the cusp of your 6th house of health from early June on. Be patient with yourself about reaching fitness goals. Gentle and steady exercise will facilitate wellness. Be aware

SPIRITUALITY

You have a strong dose of wanderlust in your heart. Pilgrimages to sacred sites would open new levels of spiritual awareness. Consider options for a journey of awakening in July or February. The Native American teachings have much to offer you. Seek a Medicine Wheel ceremony, sweat lodge, pow-wow, or drum circle.

CAPRICORN

The year ahead for those
born in the sign of the Goat
December 22 to January 20

Spring dawns with Saturn, your celestial ruler, in Aries along with the Sun, Mars, and Mercury. All four form a powerful square aspect from your 4th house. Your towering ambition can either be stimulated or overwhelmed by the challenges this will pose during March and early April. As your zodiacal symbol, the Goat, suggests, you will leap over obstacles and cross rough terrain to reach new heights. The early weeks of spring offer plenty of opportunities to do so.

Put responsibility first, play by the rules, and act conservatively. A role model or authority figure could exhibit a fatal flaw. Try to be tolerant of the failings others show and like them in spite of it all. Your efforts will be rewarded just after the Full Moon on April 11. The remainder of April brings a soft Venus aspect. You will have extra time for recreation and social activities. Good humored conversations and letters restore your faith in others.

Mars is supportive late April through May 24 as it transits your sister earth sign of Taurus. You could experience a connection with the Green Man or Pan while exercising outdoors. A deeper awareness of crystals and other energy forms emanating from Earth herself facilitates healing on every level. Make a circle of special stones and crystals on your altar at the New Moon in Taurus April 26 to pursue this further. Wait until the last half of May to travel. Mercury will move into a beneficial

trine aspect then, making journeys both safe and profitable.

As the days grow long and bright in June, Venus blesses your love sector. By Midsummer Day an existing relationship develops new depths of beauty and tenderness or you could attract a new admirer. June 9 begins an important new cycle as Saturn crosses the Taurus cusp. There is an end in sight to problems which have demanded time and attention for the last couple of years. Authority figures and institutions seem more caring and helpful. The Full Moon July 9 in your own sign of Capricorn reveals the potential of a close relationship and generates psychic dreams and heightened intuition. You'll attract new opportunity during the four weeks following that lunation.

August finds Saturn turning retrograde after Lammas. As summer wanes you will realize an old responsibility or limitation isn't quite resolved. Be patient and conscientious about tying up loose ends. Have faith, and all will be well eventually. A final chapter is completed between now and the week following Yule when Saturn will turn direct again.

Neptune ducks back into your sign August 22 after a brief hitch in Aquarius. It will be conjunct your Sun through November 26. Put spiritual values above the practical. Ask questions and do research to resolve confusion. Inspirational ideas about career path can set you apart from the crowd at work. Don't be upset, though, if others have a bit of trouble truly understanding you. Neptune generates a mystique coupled with uncertainty. Be very honest.

September's eclipse in Pisces highlights your 3rd house. Study and communication bring valuable information your way. Be creative and adventurous in meeting transportation needs. The autumnal equinox brings favorable Venus and Mercury aspects to Neptune. You will solve problems well and be able to recognize the good in companions. All Hallow's Day finds the Sun, Mercury, and Venus poised in your 11th house. Charitable acts bring rewards on and just after the holiday. Devote spare time to worthwhile causes.

Venus enters your sign December 11. Complete purchases and accept invitations to celebrate Yule then. Cultural events and the arts delight you through the end of 1998 and into New Year's week of 1999. Use the magic of color and fragrance to enhance your natural beauty as the dark, short days of winter mark the start of your birthday month. Share favorite music with a new friend or family member. January 7 brings Mercury into your sign for a brief, bright two weeks. Make important calls, and purchase books. It's a lucky time to select a new car or pick up airline tickets.

The eclipses on January 31 and February 16 conjoin the financial houses in your chart. Money could come from a different source, as an established source of income disappears. Your attitude about financial matters, especially investments and material possessions, is shifting.

As January ends you are more aware of the afterlife and other planes of reality. A comforting message from a loved one in spirit could be part of this. Late January through the rest of winter, Mars in Scorpio creates a harmonious aspect in your 11th house. You can be motivated and encouraged by positive, productive friends. Involvement with organizations and worthwhile causes or political issues adds new meaning to your life.

On March 1 Saturn moves back into Taurus and begins a trine aspect in your 5th house. A feeling of lightness and hope is generated. Children will show talent and maturity. A new love or exciting new creative project is rich with promise.

HEALTH
The knees, skin, and teeth tend to be vulnerable. Plenty of calcium in your diet is a must; also consider vitamin A supplements. Soybeans, Brazil nuts, almonds, and pistachios are good choices for snacks. Sage, which has an association with longevity and wisdom as well as purification, is the ideal herb tea. Use it as incense or try sage oil for aromatherapy. Because Mercury has a link to your health sector, retrograde Mercury cycles are times to get extra rest and can bring health needs to the fore. The late winter of 1999 from Candlemas through the equinox is an especially good time for correcting bad health habits or overcoming addictions.

LOVE
The May–December tradition of romance is for you. You can find happiness with a partner who is much older or younger. Love will blossom at work or while involved in constructive projects. June 1998 marks the onset of a more promising cycle for love than you have experienced in years. From mid-December through the first week of January, Venus in your sign intensifies your charisma and attracts happiness.

FINANCE
Always the financial wizard of the zodiac, you have kept a close eye on changing trends in the world of money and investment in recent years. Eclipses in August and January–February affect your financial situation dramatically. Be receptive to new sources of income, and develop new, salable skills. Your whole concept of financial planning could shift, be aware that all growth and changes lead to improvement ultimately. Your definition of wealth is undergoing a transformation.

SPIRITUALITY
Neptune, the planet of spiritual inspiration, is just finishing a long passage through your birth sign. September through November promises insights of a spiritual nature. A meditation near Halloween would bring a deep connection with the Lord and Lady, especially if you spend time outdoors in the mountains or a pine forest. Surround yourself with stones you have collected from places of importance to you. Assemble a medicine bag of semi-precious stones and learn the legends surrounding the various crystals. This will be an invaluable spiritual aid, especially if you work with it during the week of July 9 when the Full Moon falls in your birth sign.

AQUARIUS

The year ahead for those
born in the sign of the Water-Bearer
January 21 to February 19

A powerful amalgam of scientific, progressive energies with genuine love for humanity washes over you with the vernal equinox. Venus, Uranus, and Neptune are all in your birth sign. Your altruism reaches a new pinnacle by April 5. Your inspirations can improve the quality of life for animals and human beings in need. A new and deeper understanding of what love is all about develops during the first weeks of spring. Your zodiacal ruler, Uranus, is empowered as it moves into the middle degrees of its own sign. This year will open avenues of expression you've always secretly known were possible, but never actually manifested before. There is a sense of mission and purpose coming. Your vision quest leads you to identify and seek your personal Holy Grail.

Mid-April finds Mars entering earthy Taurus and drawing your attention toward family life and other practical concerns. You might look at real estate investments or plan home improvements April 13 – May 23. Beltane brings the ability to balance lofty ideals with practical concerns.

From the last week of May through Midsummer Day, Gemini transits of first the Sun and Mars, then Mercury make harmonious trine aspects in your 5th house. Friends include you in projects which combine pleasure with serious work. You have the opportunity to become more active in a worthwhile organization. Leisure pursuits will be stimulating mentally as well as physically. With the strong air sign emphasis, a meditation on the wind or study of breathing techniques—perhaps through yoga or rebirthing—could add much to your well-being and spiritual awakening.

The bright, warm days of summer favor social activity and cultural pursuits. Venus is supportive from June 24 – July 18. You are able to crusade for the causes you are devoted to, yet find time for whimsy and friendship. Saturn, your co-ruler, starts to make its influence felt just after the Full Moon on July 9. It moves forward in Taurus until August 15. Those close to you reveal their limitations. Keep your expectations of others realistic, and you won't be disillusioned.

August marks the start of an eclipse pattern in your sign which promises much excitement—a hint comes the week of the lunar eclipse at the Full Moon in Aquarius on August 7. Be receptive to the inevitable change in the air, and all will be well in the end. August ends with elusive, mysterious Neptune retrograding out of Aquarius back into Capricorn. It will affect your 12th house through late November. Identifying real values can be something of a challenge late summer through autumn. Interpret vivid dreams which occur now figuratively, not literally. A bit of earthy protection, such as a dash of salt or a religious emblem, helps ground unwanted astral forces. Firmly tell ghostly visitors to move toward the light between autumnal equinox and Samhain.

September finds Mars in Leo in opposition to your Sun. Listen to ideas proposed by others, but don't be coerced against your better judgment by aggressive types. Keep good company. October opens with the Sun, Mercury, and Venus in your sister air sign Libra. A benevolent aspect pattern from your 9th house is felt until the 23rd.

Uranus turns direct on October 18, ending a long retrograde cycle. It's a marvelous month for travel. Consider a pilgrimage to a sacred site or visit a place of culture and beauty. Your intellectual horizons widen through exposure to studies, publications, or other learning experiences. A letter or call from afar suggests a worthwhile idea. Entries made in your journal or Book of Shadows will prove therapeutic and valuable when reviewed in the future. November accents the 10th house. You will be more visible. Welcome opportunities to speak in public or assume new responsibility.

December brings Neptune back into your birth sign, where it will remain for many years. A fey quality touches you and grows stronger by Yule. Your imagination and sensitivity will begin to inspire those less free and fortunate. Mars energizes you with a warm trine through December and most of January. You will be highly motivated during the dark, short days of winter. Your emphatic expression of ideas and warmth will win the confidence of others.

Mercury transits Aquarius from January 26 – February 12. Candlemas time finds you brimming with ideas. An old problem is solved, and you can gain deep understanding of a new subject or task. Concentrate—you will discover new mental potentials with this cycle. The week of February 16 brings an eclipse with the New Moon in your sign. You may be changed by external events. It's a time of adjustments; identify newly developing conditions.

Winter ends with Aries planets, including Jupiter, in your 3rd house. Transportation problems are solved. Short, impromptu journeys lead to unexpected delights and opportunities. Befriend a neighbor as winter wanes.

HEALTH

Temperature extremes, especially the cold, affect you profoundly. Massage of the lower legs and protective boots or stockings are a must. Your ankle area is especially vulnerable. Elevating the lower limbs can help overall circulation. Tomato and mango dishes as well as sea salt should be a part of your diet. Red clover herb tea, hot or iced, is a marvelous overall tonic. For aromatherapy, try a camphor rub or sandalwood as an oil or incense. Your health sector has a strong link with the Moon. Observe how you feel at the New and Full Moons each month for more insight into

your health. With two eclipses in your sign this year, one at a New and one at a Full Moon, health may be in your thoughts. Be aware of how health needs are changing in August and February. A new program of care and fitness could emerge by your birthday.

LOVE

Friendship is always the basis for true love in your life. You enjoy a companion who is gregarious and loves all humanity. An old tie could break and a new one emerge this year. Wait until March of 1999 before making any binding promises, though. Changes are brewing in matters of the heart. Expect luck in love in early April and in January.

FINANCE

Lucky Jupiter is in your money house until mid-February. Your cash flow will increase and standard of living will improve. All will be well if you aren't extravagant. Resist the temptation to gamble or over-extend though. Welcome extra work, and pursue opportunities. Your efforts will be rewarded by November.

SPIRITUALITY

Neptune drifts back and forth over the cusp of Aquarius and Capricorn all year as it begins a long passage through your sign. It's a time when you will seek truth and long to define goodness. Conflicts about faith begin to resolve themselves starting in December. Yule can bring a profound spiritual awakening. Arrange meaningful spiritual symbols and scented candles on your altar that night to aid enlightenment. Your birth sign has a special affinity with the study of the stars. Esoteric astrology can help you to find spiritual solace. Examine the deeper, mystical meanings of the signs, planets, and houses of the zodiac.

PISCES

The year ahead for those
born in the sign of the Fishes
February 20 to March 20

Poetic, imaginative Neptune, your ruler, hovers on the brink of a rare sign change this year. It affects the cusp of your 11th and 12th houses as it moves from Capricorn to Aquarius. Your sensitive nature has been challenged by scandals and inconsistencies in the professional world in past years. That trend is being replaced with new excitement, even a bit of glamour, in your social life. You will encounter people who have a hint of the mythical and legendary in their lives. The Pisces-born have long been associated with the world of dreams. Your dream time can help you to recognize long-range goals and select the proper group affiliations.

Spring begins with four planets in your money sector. The financial realities of life need special consideration. Mars is involved in this stellium until April 12. Don't let money matters generate anger; instead, channel energy into making constructive changes. Retrograde Mercury is also influential. Try to analyze financial patterns and habits. Break away from those which have proven counter-productive, and you can be on the road to progress by May Eve, the feast of Beltane.

May brings supportive sextile aspects from Taurus transits of the Sun, Mars, and Mercury to Jupiter, which is in the midst of a year-long passage through your sign. Luck and opportunity are two keywords of the month. New information through travel, conversations, or the media can help you to grow. It's a marvelous time to pursue educational goals and take on other challenges.

Venus is favorable from May 29 until just past Midsummer Day. Friends are receptive to your needs; ask for advice and favors. Attend a ballet, play, or other cultural event. Dwell on the beautiful, and your whole quality of life improves during the month of June.

July finds both of your rulers, Neptune and Jupiter, retrograde. Childhood memories, as well as past life issues, can affect the present. Honor the past and learn from it, but don't let it haunt you. A progressive, energetic aspect begins as Mars enters your sister water sign of Cancer on July 6. Exercise, especially in and around water, is good for you. Through mid-August creative projects and recreational interests motivate you.

As you prepare for Lammastide, Venus moves through your love sector. The end of July and first part of August bring love and pleasure. Add new treasures to a collection. Honor the inner child by enjoying toys and games.

The Full Moon eclipse on September 6 is in your birth sign conjunct Jupiter. Magical workings for growth and healing during the week before the lunation should culminate in great success. Make the most of the extra attention and faith that others have expressed in you through the end of the month. The first three weeks of October the Sun and Venus create a quincunx aspect in your 8th house. Resist temptation; seek fulfillment of wholesome desires. The positive and negative potentials of passions of every kind are evident.

During the week before All Hallow's Eve, favorable aspects between water sign planets uplift you. Your 1st and 9th houses are blessed by Venus, Mercury, Sun, and Jupiter. The holiday heightens spiritual awareness, new philosophical awakenings, and travel. Pursue expression through the spoken or written word.

In November, Mercury joins Pluto in your career sector. You may question authority and become more vocal and visible at work. Extra effort and attention to detail make the recognition positive. The month ends with Jupiter turning direct and Neptune moving forward into Aquarius. Late November and December are dynamic and full of promise. Yuletide finds you unusually energetic and purposeful. Sentiment is replaced by an affinity for all that is contemporary and progressive. Mastering new techniques and technologies helps you move forward.

1999 begins with your 11th and 12th houses highlighted. Service to those less fortunate or other types of personal sacrifice bring happiness. Pisceans have an ancient association with martyrdom. Turn this into a positive by keeping quiet about your good deeds and thinking of others first. Your good work will be rewarded when Venus enters your sign on January 28.

Candlemas through Valentine's Day promises family happiness as well as romance. Mercury moves through your sign February 12 – March 2. Confusion clears, and problems are solved. Travel is especially productive. Venus affects your 2nd house of money during the first half of March. You will enjoy earning income— business and pleasure combine harmoniously. Plan a party on the job or surprise a coworker with a small gift. Happiness you generate in others will be returned threefold and more as winter ends.

HEALTH
Your birth sign has a unique association with the feet. Dance or exercising to music can help you stay fit, but always wear comfortable shoes. Foot massage, pedicures, and reflexology can enhance your overall well-being. If tired, try soaking your feet in epsom salts. Jupiter in your birth sign until early February gives you more resistance than usual to contagious illnesses; however, you must monitor your weight carefully. Jupiter means expansion, and extra pounds can pile up if you don't count calories. Mars in Cancer during July and August brings unusual energy, and you can overcome your usual inertia. Always have plenty of iron-rich foods in your diet such as raisins, spinach, and molasses. Drink ginseng herb tea for strength and vigor. White ginger is a healing aromatherapy treatment. You will respond especially well to spiritual healing such as *reiki* near the lunar eclipse in Pisces on September 6. Monitor health conditions carefully then.

LOVE
You must be careful of involvement in love triangles or associations with those who have addictive tendencies. Letting go of a destructive love which doesn't bring you joy is often a prelude to finding true happiness. Venus is favorable April 6 through May Eve, as well as at the end of July through early August and again October 24 – November 16. Cupid should bless you with a new love connection or strengthen an existing bond during those times.

FINANCE
Patience and practicality are the keys to security this year. Saturn is clamping down in your 2nd house of money. Keep working; resist the temptation to over-extend, gamble, or take on a large debt load and all will be well. The last half of November brings favorable energies from Jupiter, and the financial horizon should brighten. Use discretion in acting on the advice or financial demands of others.

SPIRITUALITY
Old belief systems might not be applicable to current spiritual needs. Neptune is entering your 12th house, and there can be some confusion to overcome. Emotional support from spiritual practices is a must. Try a meditation group or prayer circle which gathers regularly. Develop your natural healing ability, perhaps through therapeutic touch or the use of affirmations. September and December are times when spiritual experiences can be deeply meaningful. Dreams are always a key you can use to explore the realms beyond the mundane. Keep a dream journal and pursue the art of dream interpretation. You'll discover how lucid dreaming can serve to clear spiritual channels and heighten enlightenment.

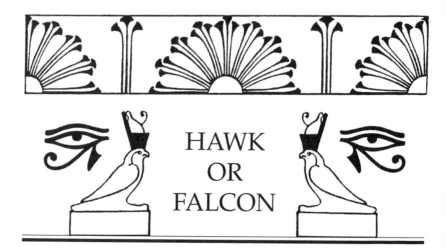

HAWK
OR
FALCON

The soaring flight of a hawk is one of nature's most thrilling sights. Early Egyptians, observing the bird's dominion of the airy realm, referred to the bird as "God of the Sky." They named the hawk Horus and worshipped him before the dynasties began, believing that this bird's quality defined a vision of all that was worthy of respect and devotion. His right eye represented the Sun; his left, the Moon; and the stars shone in his speckled plumage. Temple priests must have tamed and tended the wild birds, for they were depicted in ancient art perched on a block without tether, free to fly as they chose.

As the culture progressed, the sun god Ra evolved into the supreme deity. But the image of the hawk persisted in Ra's symbolic figure as a hawk-headed human wearing a sun disk on his head. The sky god Horus retained prestige by a mystical identification with royal

KHENSU, *the Moon*

HORUS, *the Sky*

RA, *the Sun*

Horus presents life and stability to Osiris

power, and later artists added a pharaoh's crown to the hawk image.

Centuries passed and new legends bequeathed Horus to Isis and Osiris as their son, and over time the myth extended to portray the hawk god as the heroic avenger of his father. In Egypt, the hawk remained a spiritual presence in the sacred precincts of the temple, too revered a creature to be used for sport. The 5th-century B.C. Greek historian Herodotus visited Egypt and noted: "For killing a hawk, whether deliberately or not, the punishment is inevitably death." The hawk was the primary symbol of honor, dignity, and supremacy for over the three thousand years of ancient Egyptian culture.

Hunting with birds of prey originated in China around 2000 B.C., spreading westward to India, Arabia, and Persia over a long passage of time. The returning Crusaders introduced the hunting tradition to Europe and the British Isles, where it found great favor within the royal courts.

The words "falcon" and "hawk" are used interchangeably, but in the sport of falconry sharper distinction is drawn. The hawk is short winged with bright yellow eyes; the falcon long winged with dark eyes. The bird favored by hunters is the female peregrine falcon. She is larger and more powerful than the male, as is the case with all the birds of this particular species.

But it isn't necessarily the hunter going forth with a hooded bird on his gauntleted wrist who experiences the richest pleasure of falconry. That must belong to those who tame and train the noble birds. One can imagine a spiritual kinship existing between the temple priests of ancient Egypt and their medieval counterparts preparing the birds for the field. Even today, the art is practiced in isolated regions where vast open countryside exists. Great patience, determination, and an intui-

PEREGRINE FALCON

Wood engraving from *A History of British Birds* by Thomas Bewick, London, 1826.

Royal Hawking Party   Paris, 1493

tive gift are required to gain the trust and affection of wild creatures. This especially applies to hawks and falcons, by nature restless, moody birds. Long hours in darkened rooms, often late into the night, feeding and stroking the bird with a feather is the centuries-old method of taming. Feather-stroking is essential; oil from human skin can disturb the bird's plumage by removing a natural protective coating. A quiet meditative state, slow movement and soft words calm the bird during the process. And the reward far outweighs the effort, for the quality of an established rapport between human and bird is intensely satisfying—more than that, inspiring. A hawk inspired an English poet when he sought a creature to match the character of his beloved.

> *Merry Margaret,*
> *As midsummer flower,*
> *Gentle as falcon*
> *Or hawk of the tower.*
>
> — JOHN SKELTON
> c. 1460-1529

78

Window on the Weather

El Niño—Worldwide, ominous headlines alert millions of readers to forthcoming weather perils. The culprit—an arcane, ancient and naturally recurring oceanic phenomenon called "El Niño."

Born in the Pacific off the Peruvian coast, an El Niño episode typically lasts 16 months and determines crops and weather globally. Though these unusually warm waters were previously undetected, they have profoundly affected the earth's climate and ecosystems for millions of years.

While El Niño is a hidden force, it has recently become prominent to the point of mania. In our estimation this is the result of scientific conceptualization introduced to the public in exaggerated form by the media.

And in fact, much of what will result from El Niño's influence as the months pass will be good. Hurricanes will be less frequent and East Coast winters will be mild. And while the Pacific Coast will be battered, even there a silver lining exists as reservoirs and lakes are banked full and the fire season is shortened by early wet weather.

El Niño, mighty yet transient, is the force that turns the wheel of weather in the months to come.

— TOM C. LANG

SPRING

The wind blows out of the gates of
* the day,*
The wind blows over the lonely
* of heart.*

— W.B. YEATS

MARCH, 1998—The strongest El Niño event of the century will have a distinct effect on the late-winter weather pattern. Both East and West coasts will feel the brunt of several major storms. While the month will not be unusually cold, record snowfalls are possible in the mountainous territories of the West, affecting sealevel East Coast cities from the mid-Atlantic to New England.

A warm, moist persistent air flow traveling from Southern California across the deserts of the Southwest, then crossing the Gulf States as far east as Florida, will fuel several tornado outbreaks. In the summertime, tornadoes tend to break out between 4 p.m. and 8 p.m., but these winter outbreaks can occur at any hour.

Wind energy is high, and damage can occur covering parts of several states.

Warm and dry weather arrives on a nighttime balmy breeze as spring arrives early from the Northern Plains to the front range of the Rockies.

The sun was warm but the wind
* was chill.*
You know how it is with an April day
When the sun is out and the wind
* is still.*

— ROBERT FROST

APRIL, 1998—This is the month of winter's departure, the final reminder may be a heavy one-day snowfall in the mountains by midmonth. The wind courses from converging directions, sweeping from the Tennessee Valley to the Carolinas. A group of tornadoes veiled in a thunderstorm complex looms unexpectedly. Take shelter if a strong wind foretells approaching thunder.

No late-season blizzard in the Plains, but high-elevation snows remain frequent through the northern Rockies. Still, numerous valleys turn green as rivers run high.

West Coast storms remain frequent; mud slides occur and can affect interstate travel. From Washington D.C. to eastern Maine, prolonged rainy spells can be expected.

Yellow streaks in sunset sky,
Wind and day long rain are nigh.
— TRADITIONAL

MAY, 1998—In the West, we are provided sudden sanctuary from the wrath of El Niño. In floats a wisp of harbor fog, the whisper of an onshore breeze, and the tumult subsides. Recent abundant rainfall followed by golden sunshine spilling across mountain and valley bring a particularly glorious spring.

Throughout the East, folks rediscover the tranquil pleasures of the backyard hammock.

S U M M E R

Who has seen the wind?
Neither you nor I:
But when the trees bow down
*   their heads,*
The wind is passing by.
                    — CHRISTINA ROSSETTI

JUNE, 1998—El Niño's effects are fabled by now. Though Pacific storms end, strong subtropical jet stream winds carry abundant moisture through middle America. Widespread flooding is possible in the mid-Mississippi Valley.

Water temperatures will continue above normal near the California coast. Surfers will enjoy 75 degree ocean waters.

Bands of severe local storms cause localized property damage in the Ohio Valley and central New England. A destructive major tornado will make national headlines.

Do business with men when the
*   wind's from the northwest.*
                    — BENJAMIN FRANKLIN

JULY, 1998—Fierce heat and humidity are centered through the country's midsection for much of July. Relief is found only near the immediate Atlantic and Pacific coastlines. From mid-Atlantic to eastern Maine, thick fog limits marine travel until noon, when warmer offshore winds prevail.

On occasion, violent thunderstorms traverse the Canadian border. They move quickly, carried by strong high altitude jet stream winds. Cooler air can briefly follow. These pleasant incursions will be of short duration. In most places, the month of July is hot.

Don't go back to sleep.
The wind at dawn has secrets to tell.
                    — RUMI

AUGUST, 1998—Summers' Dog Days are highlighted by subtle weather changes, the result of El Niño's end. An oscillation toward cooler Pacific waters, the "La Niña" effect, has a profound impact in the tropical Atlantic, where an early start to the hurricane season looms. The Gulf Coast is particularly vulnerable from Texas to the Florida panhandle. A strong hurricane may form in the Bay of Campeche near Yucatan or farther east in the Gulf of Honduras. Stagnant weather blankets the remainder of the nation. Air mass thunderstorms are frequent in the deep South, while the monsoon season brings isolated flash flooding to the Rocky Mountain states.

AUTUMN

Many can brook the weather that
*   love not the wind.*
                    — SHAKESPEARE

SEPTEMBER, 1998—Amber fields, bountiful harvests and lengthening shadows denote a time of transition. Evenings are luminous, clear and cool, days are balmy. Enjoy the serenity; foreboding weather will follow in about 90 days. Gathering Arctic air portends an icy winter east of the Rockies.

Three major hurricanes form in the Atlantic. One of this magnitude threatens the East Coast. Chances for a severe hurricane striking Florida this year are one in six, a higher-than-average probability. A similar probability with a less intense hurricane exists farther north on the Atlantic Seaboard.

Listen! the wind is rising,
And the air is wild with leaves,
We've had our summer evenings,
Now for October's eves.
                    — HUMBERT WOLFE

OCTOBER, 1998—A quiet time to reflect on summer's passing is accented by misty mornings' light breezes and the gradual change of seasons. Fiery reds are observed as northern maples signal the first change of foliage. Early in the month frost is confined to sheltered interior valleys of the north.

Strong mountain-borne winds descend to the outskirts of California cities and perilous wildfires result. These Santa Ana winds can exceed 60 miles per hour and danger can spread swiftly.

Peak foliage change occurs near East Coast communities by the 31st. October weather there is peaceful and the hurricane threat is over.

O wild West Wind, thou breath of
*   Autumn's being,*
Thou, from whose unseen presence the
*   leaves dead*
Are driven, like ghosts from an
*   enchanter fleeing.*
                    — SHELLEY

NOVEMBER, 1998—A bracing Arctic breeze signals winter's earliest stirring. Morning dew turns frosty at the Mason-Dixon line just before Thanksgiving. This represents an orderly cool-

82

down after warmth-giving El Niño.

Storms are confined to northern coasts, East and West, with windswept rains lashing major cities from Washington to Boston. The third week is a likely time for such weather. A brief change to snow will signal the storm's end.

Indian summer brings a week of welcome warmth to the nation's heartland at midmonth.

countryside will sparkle as storm clouds part and sunshine returns by the New Year. In its heartland, the nation's weather is quiescent for much of the month.

Winds that change against the sun
And winds that bring the rain are one.
— TRADITIONAL

JANUARY, 1999—Mighty El Niño fades back beneath the Pacific, and the January storm pattern reverts to normal frequency. In the Great Lakes area, air slightly colder than usual is entrenched. Chinook winds are due in Denver; be forewarned, the gloomy tend to feel gloomier under the influence of these eerie winds.

On the East Coast, from Virginia to New England, weather will be mild and relatively dry. The fabled January thaw will be lengthy.

You don't need a weatherman to
know which way the wind blows.
— BOB DYLAN

FEBRUARY, 1999—February snow is sparse throughout the East Coast. The storm centers flow from the Appalachian Mountains through the Alleghenies. West of this storm track, snowfall is more bountiful, with wet snowfalls changing to soaking rains sweeping the East Coast.

As El Niño's grip eases in the East, in the West this century's potentially most stormy pattern slowly ebbs.

WINTER

Welcome, wild Northeaster!
Shame it is to see
Odes to every zephyr;
Ne'er a verse to thee.
— CHARLES KINGSLEY

DECEMBER, 1998—With lengthening nights, winter's chill deepens north of the U.S. border. Minor Arctic air masses spill south. Only a few days of frigid weather are likely in the Ohio Valley and Great Lakes region early December. A more forceful surge brings long lasting cold to all the East a week before Yule time.

At month's end a fierce Atlantic coastal storm will bring ice and snow; holiday travel is hazardous. Still, the

PARSLEY   **SAGE**

𝕽𝖎𝖉𝖉𝖑𝖊 𝕾𝖔𝖓𝖌

Some of us heard this song for the first time in the sixties, when the beautifully haunting version by Simon and Garfunkel became popular. Few realized that it derived from an ancient Norse folk ballad. Over centuries, the song had become a traditional favorite throughout England with many variations, often the case with music passed down orally. The earliest printed version appeared in 1670 as "A discourse betwixt a young Woman and the Elfin Knight." Later sources (and it is included in most scholarly collections) termed it "a riddle song with many variants." Riddles, a literary form beloved by the folk of northern Europe, are a series of metaphors which challenge solving. This is clearly the point of the song we know as "Scarborough Fair." The opening stanza, authorities believe, was probably added later by ballad singers to set the scene, because it changed according to where the song was performed. William Chappell in *Old English Popular Music*, London, 1893, informs us that: "Scarborough might become Whittingham, or any other town the reciter chooses to name that is best known to him."

O, where are you going? To Scarborough fair,
Parsley, sage, rosemary, and thyme;

ROSEMARY   **THYME**

Remember me to a lass who lives there,
For once she was a true love of mine.

The Elfin Knight addresses a maiden:

> *Can you make me a cambrick shirt,*
> *Parsley, sage, rosemary, and thyme,*
> *Without any seam or needlework?*
> *And you shall be a true lover of mine.*
>
> *Can you wash it in yonder well,*
> *Parsley, sage, rosemary, and thyme,*
> *Where never spring water, nor rain ever fell?*
> *And you shall be a true lover of mine.*
>
> *Can you dry it on yonder thorn*
> *Parsley, sage, rosemary, and thyme,*
> *Which never bore blossom since Adam was born?*
> *And you shall be a true lover of mine.*

Aubrey Beardsley, 1894

The maiden replies:

Now you have ask'd me questions three,
Parsley, sage, rosemary, and thyme,
I hope you'll answer as many for me,
And you shall be a true lover of mine.

Can you find me an acre of land,
Parsley, sage, rosemary, and thyme,
Between the salt water and the sea sand?
And you shall be a true lover of mine.

Can you plow it with a ram's horn,
Parsley, sage, rosemary, and thyme,
And sow it all over with one pepper corn?
And you shall be a true lover of mine.

Can you reap it with a sickle of leather,
Parsley, sage, rosemary, and thyme,
And bind it all up with a peacock's feather?
And you shall be a true lover of mine.

When you have done and finish'd your work,
Parsley, sage, rosemary, and thyme,
Then come to me for your cambrick shirt,
And you shall be a true lover of mine.

William and Ceil Baring-Gould's *The Annotated Mother Goose*, New York, 1962, provides us with clues to help solve the riddle contained in the Elfin Knight's three questions. "In earlier days, a man who asked a girl to make him a shirt was, in effect, asking for her hand in marriage. If the girl made him the shirt, she signified that she would accept him as a "suitor."

Another note by the Baring-Goulds refers to a 14th-century fairy tale wherein a king vows to wed any maiden who can make him a shirt from three square inches of fine linen. We can deduce that the "cambrick shirt" is a tiny amulet, a love sachet. Cambric is a finely woven white linen and a square of three inches indicates a pouch to hold herbs. To wash it in a covered well and dry it on a sacred thorn bush, possibly a hawthorn, are symbolic acts of witchery. As needlework is forbidden, the pouch is secured with a ribbon or perhaps a strand of scarlet wool. The Baring-Goulds suggest that the herbs named in the refrain all have magical significance and "may stem from a witch's incantation."

As for the herbs and their sequence in the song, parsley is naturally first due to its long period of germination. Medieval gardeners planted it on the

edge of an herb garden along with rue, another plant slow to appear above ground. The practice gave rise to the expression, "We are only at the parsley and rue," meaning an enterprise talked about but not begun.

Sage is associated with long life and good health. Young wives are advised to "take a quantitie of the juice of sage, with a little salt, for four days before they company with their husbands, it will help them not only to conceive, but to retain the birth without miscarrying."

Rosemary is favored for love charms and as Willliam Langham comments in *The Garden of Health*, 1579: "Seethe much rosemary, and bathe therein to make thee lusty, lively, joyfull, likeing and youngly."

Shakespeare in *A Midsummer Night's Dream* places the proud Titania, Queen of the Fairies, on "a bank whereon the wild thyme blows," a perfect setting for dalliance.

A pinch of each of the four dried herbs combine to make an unforgettable scent—unique and compelling.

The second part of the riddle song, rich in earthy and erotic flavors, remains a puzzle. Folklorist and scholar Joseph Ritson in 1794 called it a "little English song sung by children and maids." This being so, the chances that the lyric suffered from severe editing is more than likely. Nevertheless, the maiden seems to ask for the assurance of a home, mortal love, perhaps a child and help in its rearing—practical considerations all. Romance and magic must wait until the maiden's requirements are fulfilled. A paradox—the romantic knight pays court to the sensible woman.

FULL MOON NAMES

Students of occult literature soon learn the importance of names. From Ra to Rumpelstiltskin, the message is clear— names hold unusual power.

The tradition of naming full Moons was recorded in an English edition of *The Shepherd's Calendar*, published in the first decade of the 16th century.

Aries - Seed. Sowing season and symbol of the start of the new year.

Taurus - Hare. The sacred animal was associated in Roman legends with springtime and fertility.

Gemini - Dyad. The Latin word for a pair refers to the twin stars of the constellation Castor and Pollux.

Cancer - Mead. During late June and most of July the meadows, or meads, were mowed for hay.

Leo - Wort. When the sun was in Leo the worts (from the Anglo-Saxon *wyrt*-plant) were gathered to be dried and stored.

Virgo - Barley. Persephone, virgin goddess of rebirth, carries a sheaf of barley as symbol of the harvest.

Libra - Blood. Marking the season when domestic animals were sacrificed for winter provisions.

Scorpio - Snow. Scorpio heralds the dark season when the Sun is at its lowest and the first snow flies.

Sagittarius - Oak. The sacred tree of the Druids and the Roman god Jupiter is most noble as it withstands winter's blasts.

Capricorn - Wolf. The fearsome nocturnal animal represents the "night" of the year. Wolves were rarely seen in England after the 12th century.

Aquarius - Storm. A storm is said to rage most fiercely just before it ends, and the year usually follows suit.

Pisces - Chaste. The antiquated word for pure reflects the custom of greeting the new year with a clear soul.

Libra's Full Moon occasionally became the Wine Moon when a grape harvest was expected to produce a superior vintage.

America's early settlers continued to name the full Moons. The influence of the native tribes and their traditions is readily apparent.

AMERICAN	Colonial	Native
Aries / April	Pink, Grass, Egg	Green Grass
Taurus / May	Flower, Planting	Shed
Gemini / June	Rose, Strawberry	Rose, Make Fat
Cancer /July	Buck, Thunder	Thunder
Leo / August	Sturgeon, Grain	Cherries Ripen
Virgo / September	Harvest, Fruit	Hunting
Libra / October	Hunter's	Falling Leaf
Scorpio / November	Beaver, Frosty	Mad
Sagittarius / December	Cold, Long Night	Long Night
Capricorn / January	Wolf, After Yule	Snow
Aquarius / February	Snow, Hunger	Hunger
Pisces / March	Worm, Sap, Crow	Crow, Sore Eye

YEAR OF THE TIGER
January 28, 1998 to February 16, 1999

Dark of the Moon in the zodiac sign of Aquarius marks Chinese New
Year. January 28th of 1998 saw the arrival of a Year of the Tiger,
celebrated with fireworks, wild drumming, and the clash of cym-
bals—an appropriate greeting for a year bound to be explosive,
exciting, and challenging.

It is said that a Tiger Year brings out the best in everyone.
Spontaneity is in the air. Spirits rise in anticipation, for the year
ahead promises clarity and beneficial change.

Eastern astrological years run in cycles of twelve. If you were
born on or after the Aquarian New Moon in one of the following
years, you can expect to enjoy renewed courage and vitality during
the ninth Tiger Year of the 20th century.

1902   1914   1926   1938   1950   1962   1974   1986   1998

THE CELTIC TREE CALENDAR

Beth (Birch)	December 24 to January 20
Luis (Rowan)	January 21 to February 17
Nion (Ash)	February 18 to March 17
Fearn (Alder)	March 18 to April 14
Saille (Willow)	April 15 to May 12
Uath (Hawthorn)	May 13 to June 9
Duir (Oak)	June 10 to July 7
Tinne (Holly)	July 8 to August 4
Coll (Hazel)	August 5 to September 1
Muin (Vine)	September 2 to September 29
Gort (Ivy)	September 30 to October 27
Ngetal (Reed)	October 28 to November 24
Ruis (Elder)	November 25 to December 22

December 23 is not ruled by any tree for it is the "day" of the proverbial "year and day" in the earliest courts of law.

THE WAY OF THE MOON

A New Moon rises with the Sun,
Her waxing half at midday shows,
The Full Moon climbs at sunset hour,
And waning half the midnight knows.

NEW	1999	FULL	NEW	2000	FULL
January 17		January 1/31	January 6		January 20
February 16		February None	February 5		February 19
March 17		March 2/31	March 6		March 19
April 15		April 30	April 4		April 18
May 15		May 30	May 4		May 18
June 13		June 28	June 2		June 16
July 12		July 28	July 1/31		July 16
August 11		August 26	August 29		August 15
September 9		September 25	September 27		September 13
October 9		October 24	October 27		October 13
November 7		November 23	November 25		November 11
December 8		December 22	December 25		December 11

Life takes on added dimension when you match your activities to the waxing and waning of the Moon. Observe the sequence of her phases to learn the wisdom of constant change within complete certainty.

THE WITCHES' QUARTERLY

This quarterly newsletter appears at each change of season: the Vernal Equinox (March 21st,) Summer Solstice (June 21st,) the Autumnal Equinox (September 21st,) and Winter Solstice (December 21st.) Each issue boasts a myriad of special features including an astrological forecast for each day, myths, useful information about plants and animals, and rituals and lore to help celebrate the passing seasons. Available by subscription. 12 pages. Mailed in a discreet envelope.

Subscription rates:

1/2 year (two seasons) $16.00

1 year (four seasons) $28.00

To order: Send your name and address along with a check or money order payable in U.S. funds to: Witchery Company, PO Box 4067, Middletown, RI, 02842

New titles from The Witches' Almanac

MOON LORE

As both the largest and the brightest object in the night sky, and the only one to appear in phases, the Moon has been a rich source of myth for as long as there have been myth-makers.

Elizabeth Pepper's *Moon Lore* is a compendium of lunar tales, charms, chants, and curses from ancient time to the present.

LOVE FEASTS

Creating meals to share with the one you love can be a sacred ceremony in itself. With the witch in mind, culinary adept Christine Fox offers magical menus and recipes for every month in the year.

For ordering information, turn the page.

THE MOON CALENDAR

The same calendar that appears annually in *The Witches' Almanac*, indicating the phase and place of the Moon at a glance, is now being offered as a wall calendar. Size 8½ by 11 inches, printed in rich color on fine vellum stock— available in limited numbers.

CELTIC TREE MAGIC

Robert Graves in *The White Goddess* writes of the significance of trees in the old Celtic lore. *Celtic Tree Magic* is an investigation of the sacred trees in the remarkable Beth-Luis-Nion alphabet; their role in folklore, poetry, and mysticism. Richly illustrated as you've come to expect from our publications.

A BOOK OF DAYS

A delightful book for friends of all ages. Here are 1700 gemlike quotations dealing with all aspects of human life, drawn from every source imaginable—from earliest records to the present, from Aristotle to Thurber. Quotations begin with Spring and Youth, then to Summer and Maturity, on to Autumn and Harvest, then Winter and Rest. Illustrated with over 200 medieval woodcuts.

LOVE CHARMS

Love has many forms, many aspects. Ceremonies performed in witchcraft celebrate the joy and the blessings of love. This is the theme of Elizabeth Pepper's *Love Charms*. It's a collection of love charms to use now and ever after.

RANDOM RECOLLECTIONS Vol's. I, II, III, IV.

Pages culled from the original (no longer available) issues of *The Witches' Almanac*, published annually throughout the 1970's, are now available in a series of tasteful booklets. A treasure for those who missed us the first time around; keepsakes for those who remember.